IT'S
YOUR
FUNERAL!

# IT'S YOUR Funeral!

PLAN the CELEBRATION of a LIFETIME— BEFORE it's TOO LATE

Kathy Benjamin

## QUIRK BOOKS

PHILADELPHIA

To Mommy

Library of Congress Cataloging-in-Publication Data
Names: Benjamin, Kathy, author.
Title: It's your funeral! : plan the celebration of a lifetime—
before it's too late / Kathy Benjamin.
Description: Philadelphia : Quirk Books, 2021. | Includes index. |
Summary: "A practical guide to planning your funeral, including
worksheets and guided journal prompts"—Provided by publisher.
Identifiers: LCCN 2021009711 (print) | LCCN 2021009712 (ebook) |
ISBN 9781683692584 (hardcover) | ISBN 9781683692959 (epub)
Subjects: LCSH: Funeral rites and ceremonies—United States—Planning |
Funeral service—United States—Planning.
Classification: LCC GT3203 .B46 2021  (print) |
LCC GT3203  (ebook) | DDC 393/.930973—dc23
LC record available at https://lccn.loc.gov/2021009711
LC ebook record available at https://lccn.loc.gov/2021009712

ISBN: 978-1-68369-258-4
Printed in China
Typeset in Adobe Garamond Pro and Freight Sans

Designed by Andie Reid
Illustrations by Annelise Capossela
Production management by John J. McGurk

Quirk Books
215 Church Street
Philadelphia, PA 19106
quirkbooks.com

10 9 8 7 6 5 4 3 2 1

# THIS BOOK BELONGS TO

# CONTENTS

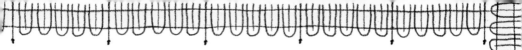

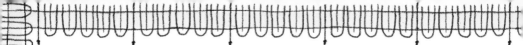

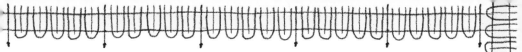

# An Introduction to Your End

**A**ccording to the National Funeral Directors Association, the average funeral today costs over $10,000. That's such a ridiculous amount of money that if you weren't already dead, the shock of it might kill you. It's enough to make you understand if your relatives chose to just dump your body in a field under cover of darkness. Yet, despite the expense, few people plan their funerals ahead of time. This is a disaster waiting to happen.

What other event of such magnitude do people drop Benjamins galore on with no arrangements in place? Weddings, vacations, births of children, car purchases: most of us prepare for months, if not years, for such milestones. But none of those are sure to be a one-off. You could have any number of marriages. Dozens of vacations. Dozens of cars. Dozens of . . . children, God help you. With a funeral, you pretty much get one shot to nail it.*

But this defining moment of your existence (or nonexistence, as it were), the one chance for your friends and family to come together and remember who you were, what they loved about you, and how you left your mark on the world, is an afterthought. No, worse—it's an anti-thought, something many people avoid thinking about completely. This isn't healthy. You are going to be worm food one day, and it's time to deal with it.

Which brings us to Nicolas Cage. Everyone loves Nicolas Cage. His films have made five billion dollars. He's got an Oscar. He named his son after Superman. Yes, he blew his fortune acquiring such esoteric items as a dinosaur skull, a pet octopus, and not one but *two* castles, but what's important is that in the middle of his spending spree, he realized he could not take any of it with him.

One of Cage's many purchases was a nine-foot-tall pyramid tomb in a famous New Orleans cemetery. It's gleaming white and engraved with the Latin phrase OMNIA AB UNO (Everything from One). Still only in his mid-forties, he'd decided to take charge of his own afterlife in the most Nicolas Cage manner possible. No way was he letting his busload of ex-wives bury him under a simple tombstone. He

---

* Unless part of your plan involves coming back to life (see "Cryonics," page 38).

looked death in the face and said, "I was Ghost Rider. Did you see that movie? It was absolutely murdered by the critics. Which I think was unfair because—anyway, my point is, you do not scare me."

You need to be at least as rational as Nicolas Cage when it comes to planning your funeral. That is a very low bar. If the star of the direct-to-DVD film *Vengeance: A Love Story* has put his affairs in order, it's time to get serious.

But not too serious. Because planning the biggest event of your afterlife should be a blast. A *fun*-eral, if you will. Within the pages of this book, you have the chance to make sure your send-off is exactly what you want it to be, whether that's a drunken bacchanalia or a sober, somber reflection on just how great you were. The decisions to make are many, as are the pitfalls to avoid. Every stage of the legacy-planning process will be considered, from selecting a burial outfit and accessories to choosing a funeral theme. Guided-journal elements and worksheets will not only help you think outside the coffin, but ensure that your wishes are recorded—which will be a massive help to your loved ones.

Just imagine: your mourners screw up your send-off because they have to throw together a five-figure event in a couple of days while sobbing uncontrollably. Having a plan will both ensure that you get the funeral of your dreams *and* take the burden of major decisions off them.

If all of this sounds too sad or scary to contemplate, it's okay. You're not alone. Take comfort in knowing that the best way to conquer your fears and anxiety about death is to face it head-on. Although you can't choose the time or manner of your demise, at least you can make sure you have a say in what happens after. By working out the details in advance, you won't have to cross your fingers that your spirit will find a way to communicate your funeral wishes through a psychic. And doesn't that make you feel just a little bit better?

Planning your own funeral is an act of love, an important aspect of positive mental health, and—thanks to this book—it's going to be a heck of a lot of fun.

# A Brief History of Funerals

Humans have been dying pretty much from the minute they started living. That's kind of how it works. Every *Homo sapiens* who ever lived has had to deal with being buried or burying other people (and often both). This means that funerals are as old as the human race itself. For at least one hundred thousand years, humans have been reinventing the funeral again and again. Sure, the main idea has been the same: get rid of the decomposing body (although, as you will learn, even how we accomplish that has changed with the times). It's generally accepted that every funeral is made up of three major ingredients: the burial, a ceremony or ritual that accompanies the burial, and a memorial or marker for the dead. But within those confines, funerals are unimaginably diverse, with every culture and era putting its own stamp on this event.

It's hard to pinpoint the earliest known funerals. After all, the only thing that makes a funeral different from just dumping a corpse in a hole is the ritual surrounding it. The majority of ancient funerary traditions haven't been preserved in the archaeological record, and so are lost to time. But we do know some things about the earliest funerals. As of 2020, the oldest known ritual burials—dating back 92,000 years—can be found in the Qafzeh cave in Israel. The twenty-seven individuals whose remains are in the cave include some of the earliest examples of anatomically modern human beings outside Africa. Some of the bodies were buried with deer antlers in their hands. Traces of ocher were also found on the bones. A child's arms had been carefully folded before his burial. Just like today, it seems that our earliest *Homo sapiens* ancestors weren't just looking to get rid of weird Uncle Terry because his body was starting to smell. They also wanted to honor Terry as he would have wanted: with his bitchin' collection of deer antlers.

Over time, funerals became way more elaborate than just burying some antlers with a body. Take the ancient Romans. According to the *Ancient History Encyclopedia*, the ideal Roman funeral required mimes, musicians, actors dressed up like the dead person's ancestors, and women who were paid to wail while literally tearing out their hair. (If you think paying people to cry over your dead body sounds like a great idea, see "Rent-a-Mourner," page 106.) All these people paraded through the streets, making noise and being conspicuous, before the deceased's body was cremated on a pyre. Some historians believe that gladiator fights originated at funerals, where wealthy families forced slaves or freelance warriors to fight to the death over the grave, believing that their blood would purify the deceased's soul. For hundreds of years, these were considered the standard must-haves.

Not everything our ancestors did would be so reviled today, fortunately. To house their many cremation urns, the ancient Romans built vault-lined structures called columbaria (singular columbarium) that we still use today. Elaborate ancient mausoleums, like the Egyptian pyramids and the Taj Mahal, are precursors to the much simpler mausoleums you see in any ordinary cemetery. And if you stood with a Paleolithic ancestor over a grave, you would both recognize the difficult mix of feelings that come from losing someone close to you.

In the Western world, the word *funeral* probably conjures up images of coffins, gravestones, embalmed bodies, and black clothing. It might seem like these aspects of funerals are eternal and immutable, but in fact they are relatively recent developments. Western rituals around funerals are strongly rooted in Victorian, Christian tradition. The Victorians were obsessed with death, and over the course of a century they bent the practice of funerals and mourning to their iron will. It's taken a long time for Western cultures to break away from those customs, even slightly. But in the grand scheme of human history, the Victorians are just a Johnny-come-lately to the business of death.

These days, funereal traditions and the funeral industry are evolving rapidly. Many of the changes, especially in North America, have been spurred by the so-called death positive movement. The term *death positive* was coined by Caitlin Doughty, a mortician, author, and host of the popular Ask a Mortician YouTube channel. It describes an attitude toward death and funerals that is centered on open and honest discussion about dying and end-of-life options. The death positive movement encourages us to look at kicking the bucket from a different perspective. Sure, one's inevitable demise might not be the best conversation topic at a coworker's retirement party, but it's definitely something you should be talking about with those closest to you. Death is a natural and inevitable part of life, and being death positive just means acknowledging that reality. The goal of this cultural openness and acceptance of death is to give people more control over their own deaths and funerals, to create more end-of-life options (especially environmentally friendly options), and to decrease anxiety and fear about death.

By being open to the idea of planning your own funeral, you are embracing death positivity. You've taken the first step in accepting your mortality and recognizing that you, too—like everyone else—will one day be attending a funeral as the guest of honor, and there is nothing you can do about it. Hopefully you will start to see that as a positive thing, or at least not a negative.

If you still feel scared and anxious about planning your funeral, that's totally normal. It might be comforting to know that you aren't going it alone. Indeed, funerals are essentially the cumulative attempts of hundreds of generations of humans to deal with those same scary and painful feelings. By wrestling with those feelings now, you'll have not only a more pleasant life but also an absolutely kickass funeral. No offense to every other human who ever lived, but your funeral is going to be the most important one of all time. Can you leave something like that to chance? Of course not! So let's start planning.

"Funerals are the rituals we create to help us face the reality of death, to give us a way of expressing our response to that reality with other persons, and to protect us from the full impact of the meaning of death for ourselves. Some funerals fulfill these functions beautifully. Others fail."

—ALLA BOZARTH CAMPBELL, author of *Life Is Goodbye,*
*Life Is Hello: Grieving Well through All Kinds of Loss*

PART ONE

# IT'S YOUR

# YOUR

# Body

# BURIAL and BEYOND
## FROM SIX FEET UNDER TO SIXTY MILES UP

The most inconvenient thing about death (other than, you know, dying) is that you won't just float away when you go. Your essence, or soul, will suddenly cease to be here on Earth, but your body will remain as, well, remains. And a body is not very pleasant once the person who inhabited it is gone.

This means that once you die, there will be a mad rush to get your body taken care of. If you want to be disposed of in a more traditional way, such as burial or cremation, the process is straightforward. No matter where you drop, there will likely be a place close by that can fulfill your wishes on short notice.

But there are many other possibilities for what to do with your remains. You might want to opt for a greener alternative, or one that's less expensive or more fun than the norm. Some of these require advanced planning. You'll want to think about costs, permits, and logistics, even for the most common body disposal options. So let's take a look at the many ways you can choose to lay yourself to rest, even when that involves absolutely no laying and a lot less rest than you might think.

# Common Methods

Ground burial and cremation are the bread and butter of the funeral industry, with more than 90 percent of Americans choosing one of these methods, according to the National Funeral Directors Association.

## GROUND BURIAL: *Going Down*

This is the classic body disposal technique. Humanity was practicing it at least 100,000 years ago. (We shouldn't be smug, though. Neanderthals had us beat by 30,000 years.) Over time, humans perfected the burial process, eventually realizing that dead bodies are best kept away from habitations—that is, buried in cemeteries—and deposited deep enough so they wouldn't reemerge due to flooding or hungry animals. Then came coffins, which protect the body from the elements; they can be as simple as a wooden box or as elaborate as King Tut's golden sarcophagus.

In modern times, the body is sometimes embalmed before burial. The modern chemical embalming process originated in the mid-1700s, but it wasn't until a plethora of corpses found themselves far from home in the 1860s thanks to the Civil War that embalming became de rigueur in the United States. To this day, in a traditional ground burial, the body is usually conserved in this manner, and if you want an open casket funeral, embalming is a must. (If you're more interested in going au naturel, see "Natural Burial," page 29.) This process isn't for the dead person but rather for the living. If the body looks pristine, with no signs of decay or other unpleasant effects of death, mourners can say their final goodbyes to a person who looks just as they remember them. And it may even be beneficial: seeing the body of the deceased helps jump-start the grieving process for many mourners.

Be aware that embalming is a hardcore process. Essentially, your body is desecrated just to make it look nice. And the tricks used to do that are pretty barbaric. To spare you the nightmares, we won't go into the full details (though if you're truly interested, Caitlin Doughty explains "What Happens to a Body During Embalming?" on her Ask a Mortician YouTube channel). Instead, here's just one technique for getting the face to look angelically peaceful, according to the website of the nonprofit organization Funeral Consumers Alliance: "Facial features are set by putting cotton in the nose, eye caps below the eyelids, and a mouth-former in the mouth, with cotton or gauze in the throat to absorb purging fluids. The mouth is then tied shut with wire or sutures. Glue may be used on the eyelids or lips to keep them closed in an appropriate pose." Lovely.

If you're willing to put your body through embalming for the comfort of your family, that is a noble thing. But if you're grossed out right now and don't want embalming fluid coming anywhere near you, there's good news! If you plan on being buried with your casket firmly closed, there's no need for it. Preserving a dead body is not required for safety reasons; an unembalmed corpse will not contaminate the water supply, contrary to popular belief. In fact, the toxic chemicals used in embalming are much worse for the environment than a decaying corpse. If you're looking for a green send-off, embalming is definitely not the option for you.

Burial also may not be for you if you dislike spending a lot of money (even after you're no longer on the hook for the bill). There are ways to have a funeral on a budget, and the first step is to skip ground burial entirely. Not only will you have to shell out for a burial plot, but even regular, boring coffins can cost in the five figures. Then there's the burial vault, a concrete liner that surrounds the coffin in the grave, which most cemeteries insist on and which adds a couple more zeros, as does embalming. And of course, there's a fee for "perpetual care" of your grave plot, so that even after your loved ones die, your grave will always be tended to.

The cost may be worth it if the tradition is important to you or if your religion requires it. When people imagine a funeral, they generally think of family gathered around a hole in the ground while a coffin is lowered in and covered with dirt. It's all very safe and predictable. That's not necessarily a bad thing when dealing with such a traumatic event. Sticking to traditions can make the event feel calmer and more bearable. Throwing a curveball like asking grieving loved ones to dump you on a body farm (page 43) could be too much for them to deal with. A traditional ground burial lets your mourners go through the expected motions and maybe even see your physical body one last time, which can be comforting.

# HOW TO AVOID BEING BURIED ALIVE

**A**lthough being buried alive might sound like an urban legend, there's plenty of evidence that people have gone to their graves a lot less dead than is ideal. If you're dead set on being set dead in a grave, be prepared. Not having a burial removes the possibility right off the bat. (The first man to be cremated in the United States did so partly because he'd known a woman who'd been buried alive. Not that being *burned* alive seems like a great trade-off . . .) Here are a few other fail-safes:

## BELL SAFETY COFFIN

The idea behind this Victorian invention was that if you woke up and found, to your great consternation, that you had been buried before your time, you could pull a string that would allow air to flow into the coffin, as well as ring a bell located above your grave. Someone would hear the noise and rush to dig you up. (Maybe you'd get extra lucky and grave robbers would already be in the middle of the process.)

## MODERN SAFETY COFFIN

More than a century later, inventors are still working to perfect the above. In 2014, another patent was approved, this time for a "portable alarm system" attached to the casket. All the disoriented victim needs to do is push a button, and help will arrive. Only drawback: you can expect your friends to make zombie jokes for the rest of your bonus-life.

## CELL PHONE

Will you get service down there? No. But you can play games to pass the time until you run out of oxygen. (Plus, everyone is bringing their cell phones to the grave these days. See "Cell Phones," page 58.)

# CREMATION: *From National Scandal to Business as Usual*

In 2016, *Time* magazine reported that, in the United States, cremation had surpassed burial as the most common way of getting rid of those pesky dead bodies lying around. It's now the norm in many places around the world. But while some cultures have been down with the practice for centuries, including in Japan and India, ordering your remains well-done was controversial in the Christian West until relatively recently. Modern cremations in the United States and Europe began only in the 1870s, and at the time people were apoplectic. What kind of sick freaks would want their bodies to burn? They should rot in the ground like God intended! Or so people said. The debate raged for decades, and although the Catholic Church eventually condoned the practice in 1963,* by the 1980s, cremation was still uncommon and considered slightly weird.

Yet as proponents argued from the beginning, cremation has lots of positives. Cremated remains (or cremains, as they are known) take up relatively little space, so there is no need to set aside acres of land for the use of people who can no longer appreciate it, although cremains can of course be traditionally interred.** Cremains are easy to transport. A loved one can keep your cremains in their house, spread them somewhere that meant a lot to you (but not in Disney theme parks, they frown on that), or do something special with them (see "Getting Creative with Cremains," page 24). The cremation process can even involve your loved ones. Some crematories allow the family to be present when the body is incinerated—or even to push the button that starts the procedure.

What is this procedure, exactly? In short, cremation involves a special furnace called a retort, which is heated from 1,400 to 1,800 degrees Fahrenheit. Some countries and U.S. states require a container, be it a coffin or a cardboard box, to hold the body in the retort, which is cremated along with it. (Other states have laws dictating that nothing can be put in the furnace besides the body. Confused?

---

\* The Catholic Church still regards the scattering of ashes as verboten, however, and directs that cremains must be buried.

\** *Burial* and *interment* are interchangeable terms, although these days the latter is more commonly used to refer to what you do with an urn of cremains, whether burying it or sealing it in a niche at a columbarium. Confusingly, putting the cremains into the urn itself is called *inurnment*.

See "What Can Be Cremated with Me?" page 66.) Contrary to popular belief, the body isn't actually set on fire. Instead, over the course of ninety minutes to three hours, the intense heat vaporizes virtually everything but the bones. So, if corpses aren't set alight but instead mostly vaporized, what are these so-called ashes (as they are colloquially known) that crematoriums are handing back to sad loved ones? They are actually the charred bones, which are taken from the retort and blended into powder in a machine called a cremulator. The resulting "ashes" are thicker and whiter than ash from a fire.

Another benefit to cremation is financial: a simple coffin can cost as much as a decent used car, but even the nicest urns only run into the hundreds of dollars. Finally, there's the symbolism. Sure, you might not rise from your ashes like a phoenix, but the quick, clean destruction of your remains by fire has a kind of macabre beauty to it. No messy decomposition for you. No fighting the inevitable by mutilating your corpse with embalming. Ashes to ashes, dust to dust, with rapid efficiency. Nailed it.

Unfortunately, cremation is not the most environmentally friendly exit. If you were fastidious about limiting your carbon footprint in life, you probably don't want to ruin all your hard work in death. Cremating a body the standard U.S. way is the equivalent of burning through two tanks of gas in a car, according to Nora Menkin, the executive director of People's Memorial Association, an educational and advocacy group. Plus it can release toxins, like mercury from dental fillings, into the air. It's better for the environment than sticking an embalmed body in a coffin in the ground, but if you're hoping to go out green, cremation might not be the best choice.

# GETTING CREATIVE WITH CREMAINS

**O**nce the human body has been vaporized into a (surprisingly large) pile of ash, the body disposal fun has only just begun. That's because you can do anything—literally almost anything—with human cremains. Think of the most perfect way you'd want your ashes to be used, no matter how bizarre, and someone is probably offering to do it in exchange for money. Here's a selection of interesting ideas.

## MEMORIAL DIAMONDS

Diamonds have a bad rap these days due to the horrible conditions under which many are mined. Fortunately, lab-created diamonds have stepped in to make sure the sparkler on your finger is ethically produced. That same technology also makes it possible for you to become a sparkler yourself after you die.

More than ten companies around the world offer to extract carbon from either your hair or your cremains, add additional carbon to bind it together, and turn you into a diamond. It's a lengthy process—requiring about seven to eleven months—but lightning fast compared to how long it takes a diamond to form in the Earth's mantle. Before you die, be sure to decide how big a stone you want to be, and what color. The more carbon that's derived from you in the diamond, the bluer the gem will be, but other colors are available. Costs vary depending on which options you pick and the company you go with, but be prepared to spend at least mid- to high four figures, if not more.

## BODY PAINT

If the creepy creativity of plastination (page 45) is a step too far even for your artistic soul—or if you're just more into paintings than sculpture—there are plenty of artists out there willing to make something beautiful from your ashes. In this case, they mix some of your cremains with paint and then paint a picture with it. The artists don't need a license or official permission, just a willingness to offer this service. It's no odder than most things people do with ashes, and it can be beautiful, both literally and figuratively. As one such artist named Adam Brown says, "Having ashes in an urn on a mantel somewhere is a good way to constantly remind yourself that person died, but when you use them in an artwork it's a good way to remember someone lived."

You can have anything painted with ashes, but many people choose a portrait of the deceased. If you request this method for yourself, it will be a kind of *Inception*-like situation, in which you are used to make an image of yourself but also you no longer exist. What is reality anyway, man?

## VINYL COMPRESSION

Consider this method not only for your ashes but as an investment opportunity while you are still alive. Once Millennial hipsters start dying en masse, the company And Vinyly (props to whomever came up with that name) will probably have more business than they can handle. If you would rather die than listen to music on an MP3, you can get your cremains pressed into a playable record after you actually die.

The FAQ on the company's website encourages you to make all the decisions about your record now, including artwork (which you can design yourself), track list, size, and so on. When they receive a teaspoon of your ashes, voilà! Your loved ones can listen to your vinyl mix forever, or until the record wears out. (See, MP3s do have *some* benefits. But don't worry; since this method requires so little cremains, your family can just make you into more records.)

## FIREWORKS

It was the writer Hunter S. Thompson who initially piqued people's interest in going out with a bang. His much-publicized funeral in 2005 (which cost millions and was bankrolled by actor Johnny Depp) culminated with some of his ashes being shot out of a specially designed cannon during a fireworks display, which was made up of pyrotechnics containing his ashes. In 2019, the film *Poms*, starring Diane Keaton, used memorial fireworks as a plot point. Even though you've probably never heard of that movie, some people saw it and were inspired to have their own postmortem explosion spectacular.

This option is perfect for those who love the Fourth of July or Guy Fawkes Night, veterans, or anyone who wants their funeral to be a real celebration. After all, who can be sad while watching fireworks? Putting on such a show comes with a whole bunch of regulation and permit issues, so only a few funeral homes and companies offer fireworks displays to their clients, costing a few thousand a pop. Some companies offer cheaper "self-fired" kits for home use, but be sure to research local regulations around exploding cremains if you go this route.

## A FEW MORE FOR THE ADVENTUROUS

**BECOME A TATTOO:** Imagine not just your name in a heart on your loved one's arm, but your *ashes* in your name in a heart on your loved one's arm, in a cliché and very permanent display of mourning. Yes, some tattoo parlors will mix a small bit of your ashes with ink and mark up anyone who is brave enough.

**TAKE TO THE AIR:** If you love flying, you are a crazy person. Regardless, there are plenty of companies that will spread your ashes from the air. You can even choose from classic wartime planes, either through private bookings or a company like the UK-based Fly a Spitfire, which offers a scattering service. If balloons are more your thing, Eternal Ascent Society makes 5-foot biodegradable ones in which some of your cremains can be placed, allowing you to float to the heavens until the balloon bursts and you are spread across the world. To get a bit more bang for your funeral buck, try the Loved One Launcher, a small cannon-like device that shoots your cremains up to 70 feet in the air.

**GO OUT WITH A BANG:** A company called Holy Smoke will put a small amount of your cremains in a bullet or cartridge so you can go on one last hunt. This is the perfect option if your nemesis was responsible for your demise. A loved one using a bullet made of your ashes to exact revenge is sure to get made into a blockbuster movie.

**PROVIDE A COMFORTING CUDDLE:** The problem with traditional urns is that they're so hard to hug. But what if the urn was encased within a stuffed animal? Yup, that's a thing. There are different sizes and styles of teddy, so you can pick the perfect one for your loved ones to store your cremains in and snuggle with.

# My CREMATION CREATIONS

If applicable, describe anything creative you would like to be done with your cremains. Whether you want your ashes made into a tattoo, a firework, a painting, a diamond, or all of the above, let your loved ones know here. Include directives if you'd like these cremation creations to be bequeathed to someone special. Don't worry—you can still have a traditional interment or scattering if you wish (see "My Eternal Rest," page 120). There'll be plenty of cremains to go around.

# Eco-Friendly Methods

Everyone's worried about their carbon footprint these days, and for good reason. You may wish to consider how you affect the environment not only in life, but in death as well.

## NATURAL BURIAL: *The Past Is Present*

Look, our ancestors may not have had drive-through Starbucks and drone-delivery burritos, but their simple lives were beautiful in a lot of ways. One thing they didn't overcomplicate was burial. Okay, a few built giant pyramids or assembled terracotta armies, but for most people, burial was as simple as being placed in a hole to decompose. After hundreds of years of making funerals more and more complicated, with chemicals galore and a huge list of expenses, some of us are looking back to those simpler times.

Natural burials are exactly what they sound like: a straightforward, back-to-nature disposal of your body. There's no embalming fluid or concrete burial vaults. Instead, the body is wrapped in a shroud or placed in a casket made of a material that breaks down easily, like wicker. The grave is dug shallower than a standard one, allowing your remains to mix with the aerated soil and bacteria. (Don't worry: you'll be deep enough that animals will not be able to smell you. Promise.) Your body decomposes and enriches the soil and you feed the natural world, returning the favor after it fed you for so long. (Now a pause while you sing "Circle of Life" from *The Lion King*.)

Natural burials are legal in the United States, though cemeteries set their own rules, so some might not allow this option. But there are plenty that do, and you should be able to find one in the general location where you want to be buried. You can go a step further and request to be laid to rest in a "conservation burial" cemetery, which means the land you are buried on can never be developed in the future. (Yes, old graveyards are sometimes torn up by construction equipment. Just ask any Native American.) Keep in mind that natural and conservation burial grounds restrict the types of headstones and monuments that can be used, with most allowing only wooden, plant, or natural rock markers.

# PET CEMETERIES (THE NOT-EVIL KIND)

**P**ets are the best. That's just a fact. And for many of us, the idea of being parted from our animal friends in death is extremely painful. So it's a real bummer that most cemeteries today don't allow animals to be buried alongside their humans. (Unlike in Oberkassel, Germany, where there's a double grave that dates back 14,000 years containing two humans buried with their dog.)

U.S. laws governing cemeteries vary by state, and most of those laws seem to have been enacted by evil villain pet-haters. Some people are so desperate to stay with their animals in death that they are cremated and interred with them in a pet cemetery. Fortunately, groups like the Green Pet-Burial Society are pushing for "whole family" cemeteries that allow you to be buried with your beloved companion, whether they're a cat or a bird or a horse. If heading over the rainbow bridge with your pet is important to you, be sure to look into your local laws and regulations and find out if there's a pet-friendly cemetery near you.

If you can't find a way to legally be laid to rest with your pet, there are other deeply meaningful and symbolic ways to stay close. Some of your ashes could be scattered over your pet's resting place or vice versa. You could also be buried with their collar, leash, favorite toy, or even a clay imprint of their paw.

## RECOMPOSTING: *Sure, It Sounds Gross . . .*

Okay, keep an open mind. Corpse composting seems like something the serial killer in a horror movie would do, but in fact this option is on the cutting edge of the green funeral revolution. Dead bodies decompose. It's just what happens, even if your instinct is to stick your fingers in your ears and scream "LALALALALA" when someone brings it up. Please take your fingers out of your ears. This is a book; it doesn't make noise. And we're going to discuss this like adults.

Once you accept that you're going to decompose, it's easy enough to come to terms with speeding up the process. That's the essence of corpse composting. Your body is placed in a pod or box, covered with wood chips and similar organic material, then heated to about 131 degrees Fahrenheit. Heat-loving microbes and bacteria do their thing, breaking down your body as well as killing any contagions. After thirty days (or nine months, if you want your bones included), you have become a pile of nutrient-rich compost.

Your loved ones are given the compost, which they can spread in a garden or on the roots of a tree. The chosen spot then becomes a memorial location they can visit in the future, comforted in the knowledge that your essence is literally in all of the beautiful flowers and leaves.

And that's not the only way recomposting is super green. It uses only one-eighth the energy of cremation, saving a metric ton of carbon dioxide per person, according to Troy Hottle of the U.S. Environmental Protection Agency.

As of 2020, recomposting is legal only in Washington state, but it looks like this method is going to break out in a big way. However, if you're Catholic, maybe check with your priest first. The Washington State Catholic Conference has denounced the process, deeming it undignified. Others say that since Pope Francis is big on the environment, he probably wouldn't mind. Sure, Jesus wasn't recomposted, but he kind of cheated death anyway. The rest of us need options.

## TREE BURIAL: *Turning Your Death Day into Earth Day*

If corpse composting is a bridge too far but you like the idea of helping plants grow with all that leftover energy you won't have use for once you're dead, then tree burial may be just what you're looking for.

After a standard cremation, your cremains are placed in a biodegradable urn (available from several companies, including the Living Urn and the Bios Urn) and planted with a tree sapling, which grows big and tall while getting nourishment from what's left of you. It sounds lovely, and symbolically it is. But the problem is that once you are ash, you don't really have any good nutrients left. Still, it's fine to ignore the inconvenient science for the beautiful concept. Plus, as the tree grows, your loved ones will have a peaceful place to sit and reflect on your greatness. The living, growing tree becomes a metaphor for your own life. Instead of cutting a tree down to make your coffin, you bring another tree into the world. It's poetry.

In the near future, though, your options may not be limited just to symbolically growing a tree from your remains. Capsula Mundi has designed an egg-shaped biodegradable pod meant to hold a human body in a fetal position. As the body decays, the tree feeds off it. You really can live on in the tree, "circle of life" style. The goal is to one day offer "sacred forests" full of these trees as an alternative to traditional cemeteries. The glitch is that the company experimenting with these pods is located in Italy, where natural burials of any kind are illegal. So, as of 2021, these larger body pods are only theoretical. Still, with the way green burials are trending, full-body tree pods could likely be an option for you—if you aren't in a hurry to die.

## BURIAL AT SEA: *Making Waves*

Giving your body to the deep isn't just for sailors and navy veterans anymore. Anyone can be buried at sea. So if you want to join eminent people like Janis Joplin and John F. Kennedy Jr., who are swimming with the fishes, consider this ancient form of body disposal.

Sea burial can mean either whole-body burial or the burial or spreading of cremated ashes. Whole-body sea burial is more complicated, for obvious reasons, but in the United States at least, both methods require the same permits and fall under the same rules.

First, you have to be at least 3 nautical miles out to sea (and at a depth of 600 feet, for whole bodies) before you start dumping remains, and you can't dump anything that won't decompose. The U.S. Environmental Protection Agency's list of no-nos includes "plastic or metal flowers and wreaths, tombs, tombstones, gravestones, monuments, mausoleums" (although if you manage to ship a mausoleum out to the middle of the ocean, I'll be impressed). There is plenty more red tape, and you'll need to get your hands on a boat, but don't fret. Multiple companies are ready to help make your wish come true and will even streamline the process for you.

When done correctly (as in, not by criminals trying to dispose of evidence), precautions are taken to prevent your body from washing up on a beach. Your corpse can be weighed down by a biodegradable coffin or an object if your body is only wrapped in sailcloth or canvas (a cannonball or two is traditional).

Especially if you choose not to be cremated, burial at sea can be quite a green option. Instead of nurturing plants on land, you feed animals in the sea. It's still the circle of life, except one of those lives might be a shark.

If you are a U.S. Navy veteran, another bonus is that burial at sea with a military service is free. The downside is that civilians can't attend. If your loved ones want to feel like they're a part of the ceremony, consider asking them to cannonball into a pool in your honor.

## CORAL REEF BURIAL: *Under the Sea . . . Forever*

If you like the idea of being buried at sea but want your remains to remain permanently, there's the option of becoming a coral reef. This is an increasingly popular choice for anyone who loves the ocean, is looking for an environmentally friendly exit, or just likes the idea of spending eternity near Miami.

The idea is simple: after a standard cremation, your ashes are mixed with cement and sculpted into a small structure or statue that is added to the ocean floor. Algae and diatoms build up on your memorial, then small animals like shrimp show up, followed by fish and even real coral. Researchers aren't yet sure of the full impact because the process is so new, but adding these memorials to places where reefs have been destroyed seems to bring back important marine life.

While that sounds great for the earth, if you are one of those people who puts Kermit the Frog to shame when it comes to being green, the benefits to the ocean might not be worth the other costs to the environment. Cremation uses a lot

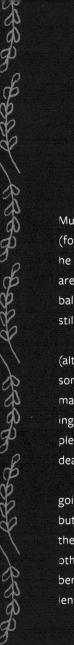

# VIEWINGS

Much of what happens concerning death is shrouded in euphemism (for example, saying that your college roommate "passed on," not that he "chugged a 40 before trying to wrestle an alligator"). But viewings are much more straightforward: mourners come by to view the embalmed body. Even if you're cremated or want a closed casket, you can still have a viewing; the idea is the same.

For many, seeing a deceased loved one is a part of finding closure (although other people may find it uncomfortable, for obvious reasons). Research indicates that viewing the body is the moment when many people accept that death has occurred and are able to start grieving, especially if the death was sudden or traumatic. It's true: many people will remain in denial until they quite literally come face-to-face with death. So it's an important occasion on the funeral calendar.

Viewings tend to be informal gatherings, with people coming and going throughout a set period. Traditionally, they took place at home, but in modern times they're often held in funeral homes. Although the person who has died takes center stage physically, as with most other events following a person's death viewings are really about the bereaved. They provide an opportunity for mourners to offer condolences to the family and say goodbye to the deceased.

of fuel, and cement plants release huge amounts of carbon dioxide into the atmosphere. But considering how badly coral reefs have been affected by climate change, and how vital they are to a healthy ecosystem, it's a trade-off worth considering.

Becoming a coral reef after you die is now so popular that there are multiple companies ready to add you to the ocean floor. Eternal Reefs adds cremains to a "Reef Ball" designed to mimic the structure of coral. You can choose to be mixed with your pet's ashes, or those of up to three other people. Alternately, the Neptune Memorial Reef off the coast of Miami can mix your cremains into slightly more interesting shapes, like bricks used to build ancient-looking ruins, or statues of lions or shells.

If you do choose this option, your family might want to learn to scuba dive. Just like on land, loved ones can visit your undersea remains, though it takes more effort. But since they're getting a nice vacation out of it, you might have relatives coming to pay their respects for generations to come.

## MUSHROOM SUIT BURIAL: *From Fun Guy to Fungi*

This is a burial option cool enough for teen heartthrob Dylan McKay. Yes, when the *90210* actor Luke Perry tragically died from a stroke at just fifty-two years old, he'd already decided what he wanted to do with his body. According to his daughter Sophie, when Perry discovered the mushroom suit, he "was more excited by [it]" than she'd ever seen him.

So what is this bizarrely named outfit? It's a loose black shirt and pants, with head, face, and hand coverings that make the wearer look like a ninja. (You can also get it in "natural," a beige color, but who would pick that when they can have the ninja option?) The organic cotton fabric is embedded with bits of mushrooms that are specially selected for the process. You are buried in the suit, with no coffin, anywhere that a natural burial is allowed. Then, as your body decays and the mushrooms grow, they draw nutrients from your corpse and spread them around the soil, helping surrounding plants. Jae Rhim Lee, founder of Coeio, the only company currently selling the suit, claims the mushrooms also help reduce toxins and pollutants, like lead and mercury, which leech out of bodies as they decompose.

Even better, the mushroom suit is also called the "infinity burial suit." Imagine mentioning at a dinner party that you're going to be buried in an infinity burial suit. You'll sound like Iron Man. Plus, it's an extremely green way to go out. Not only does your body help the environment, but Coeio promises to plant two trees for each order. If you love the idea but have other plans, you can purchase a mushroom suit for your pets.

Not everyone is a fan. When Sophie Perry posted about mushroom burial on Instagram, one notable comment read: "This is creepy, disgusting, and disturbing. Imagine now using the mushrooms for a recipe . . . mushrooms that have been feeding off a corpse." First of all, random Instagram user, all wild mushrooms feed off corpses. Animals die too, and they are good eating for fungi. Second, go sit on a thumbtack. The mushroom suit is awesome.

If the idea intrigues you but you're worried about people's reactions, just stick to calling it the infinity burial suit. Then stare off into the distance before walking away. Let them draw their own conclusions.

# Futuristic Methods

You probably don't plan on dying tomorrow (fingers crossed!), which means mortuary science has plenty of time to come up with new ways to dispose of you when you finally do give up the ghost. Since everyone dies eventually and there are more people than ever on this planet, many of whom are interested in new ways of returning to Earth or launching away from it, entrepreneurs are constantly working on the next big thing in body disposal.

## RESOMATION: *Cremation with a Twist*

Originally invented to dispose of animal carcasses quickly and cleanly, resomation was first used on human bodies at the Mayo Clinic in Minnesota in 2005. The process is technically called "alkaline hydrolysis," a term that doesn't quite have the right reverent, mournful tone. So it's a good thing that resomation is also known as "green cremation," combining two of the hottest trends in body disposal. If you want more monikers, how about aquamation, biocremation, flameless cremation, and water cremation? They're all attempts to explain that a body can be cremated without using fire.

Sort of. Your family will receive some ash-like remains back, just as if you'd been cremated, but it will be far from all of you. Here's why: Resomation involves putting your body in a special container filled with water and potassium hydroxide. This you-soup is heated to well past boiling, but because of extreme pressure inside the container, the mixture doesn't actually boil. Instead, you kind of stew for a few hours. The end product is a brown-green liquid waste that . . . um . . . gets dumped down the drain. Bye-bye, all your soft bits. Your bones remain and are then ground up into the "ash" that's given to your family.

It sort of lacks the ashes-to-ashes, rising-like-a-phoenix poetry of fire cremation, doesn't it? But one woman who chose resomation for her late husband told the BBC she liked that it had "an echo of childhood baptism," which is a lovely way to think about it. It's also great for anyone who was environmentally conscious in life or just enjoyed a good, (really, really) hot bath.

Though not yet legal in every U.S. state, resomation is an option for many Americans. Unless you live in New Hampshire, where the process was banned in 2008. Outside the United States, only Australia, Canada, and Mexico currently have a single funeral business each that offers resomation.

Despite being pooh-poohed by the Catholic Church, which asserts that stewing your corpse is not showing enough "respect and reverence" (well, when you put it like that, sure), resomation is very environmentally friendly. It produces a third less greenhouse gas than cremation and requires a seventh of the energy. If people can overcome the ick factor, its popularity will surely continue to grow. As long as words like "liquid waste" and "sludge" aren't included in the sales pitch.

## CRYONICS: *Ice, Ice, Body*

If you're reading this book, you're probably open to the idea of accepting your inevitable demise. But if you've gotten this far and decided, "Nope, this whole dying thing is really not for me," then boy are you going to love cryonics!

The cryonics business promises life after death. And not in an afterlife kind of way, where you might burn in a lake of fire or have to learn how to play the harp. In a "we're going to literally bring you back to life just as soon as we figure out how" kind of way.

Cryonics officially began on "Bedford Day," January, 12, 1967. The 73-year-old James Bedford, a plain old regular guy who just happened to be intrigued by a group called the Life Extension Society, died of cancer. A few hours later, he became the first body preserved through cryonics. Bedford's body was moved around a bit and dunked in different solutions as the science developed, but when it was checked on in 1991, it hadn't decomposed. It's still in stasis today. (Someone who is *not* in cryostasis is Walt Disney. See "There's No Dying in Baseball!," page 41.)

Some cryonics businesses have gotten bad press due to accusations of mishandling remains, so be sure to do your research before committing. Also, be aware that even in the best-case scenario, your corpse may be decapitated, with the two parts stored separately or your body not stored at all. It's cheaper to store just your head in a fluid-filled container (yes, exactly like in *Futurama*), and since part of the hypothesis of cryonics is that you'll only need your brain—to be uploaded into a computer or simulation in the future—the rest of your meat sack is just getting in the way.

If you go this route, you'll need to accept that you might spend eternity on ice. The science of cryonics is theoretical at best and a big pile of cow dung at worst. In 2015, the *MIT Technology Review* listed the many reasons cryonics will never bring someone back to life in any way, namely that the human mind and its interconnections are too ridiculously complex for it to ever be possible to replicate or reanimate. Even Alcor Life Extension Foundation, probably the most famous cryonics company, admits cryonics is "an experiment in the most literal sense of the word." Their pitch is essentially that it's worth a shot, just in case it works, right? That's an expensive gamble to take. As of 2020, the cost of preserving a body through cryonics ranged from $28,000 to $200,000. Being frozen is a one-time fee, so you don't need to worry that your great-great-granddaughter will miss a payment and your body will be defrosted. However, you do need to become a dues-paying member of the Cryonics Institute (currently $120 per year) while you are alive, which isn't included in that estimate.

## SPACE BURIAL: *The Final Frontier*

People freaking love space. It would be impossible to count how many books and movies are set among the stars. Every kid wants to be an astronaut, to blast off, see the Earth from a new perspective, and feel weightless. But it turns out that becoming an astronaut is, like, *really* hard. Thankfully, there's a loophole. If you just wait until you're dead, you can skip all those years of education and training because all you'll need to go to space is money.

Now, if money is also an issue, there are different levels of "going into space" offered by the various memorial spaceflight companies. One of the biggest is Celestis, which launched Gene Roddenberry and James "Scotty" Doohan of *Star Trek* into the final frontier, as well as hundreds of others. It offers four options for all your postmortem astro-corpse needs. (But be aware that all of Celestis's services concern "small symbolic portions" of cremains only.)

- **EARTH RISE:** *Your cremains are deposited in a capsule, launched beyond Earth's atmosphere, and then returned to your loved ones.*

- **EARTH ORBIT:** *Your ashes are launched into orbit, circling the Earth until the capsule eventually reenters the atmosphere and burns up, like a shooting star.*

- **LUNA:** *Your cremains are landed on the moon or launched into lunar orbit.*

- **VOYAGER:** *In arguably the coolest option, your ashes are put on a special spacecraft that goes on a "permanent celestial journey" into the solar system. The next launch is set for 2022, so plan your death around that if you can.*

Your loved ones can be involved in the ceremony in which you posthumously prove you're just as heroic as Neil Armstrong, either attending the launch or watching a live broadcast. If you want your beloved pet to join you in space, that's an option, too—Celestis offers the same services for animals as they do for humans. If you love space but aren't down with cremation, you can have your DNA launched instead.

If your heart is set on space burial, it's important to plan ahead due to costs, limited availability, and infrequent opportunities to blast off (some companies launch only every few years).

## THERE'S NO DYING IN BASEBALL!

No matter what you've heard, Walt Disney is not cryonically frozen underneath the Pirates of the Caribbean ride at Disneyland. Nor is his frozen body located anywhere else. He was cremated two days after he died and interred in the swanky Forest Lawn Memorial Park in California. But within weeks of his death, the rumors had started, and over the years were increasingly exaggerated, until finally his daughter stated unequivocally that her father had never requested to be frozen.

But one famous man's daughter made the opposite claim. When baseball legend Ted Williams died in 2002, two of his children produced a stained scrap of paper signed by their father that said he was interested in "Bio-Stasis." Williams's third child, however, had the athlete's will, which clearly said he wanted to be cremated. Nevertheless, Williams's remains somehow ended up at the Alcor Life Extension Foundation, with his head in one tank and his body in another. Tons of drama followed, including a lawsuit, accusations of mismanagement at the facility, and a *Sports Illustrated* exposé on the whole sorry situation.

It's still unknown what Williams's wishes were. So learn from his mistake: make sure all your loved ones know what you want done with your body after you die, especially if your choice is unorthodox. Put those wishes in writing and have them signed, dated, and witnessed. (See "Where There's a Will," page 155.)

# Donation Methods

Look, you won't be needing your body anymore, and there are plenty of people out there who could make good use of it. Organ donation is the most common way to ensure that parts of you live on after death, although there are other medical and scientific uses for every last bit of you.

## BODY DONATION: *Or, How to Get into Med School Without Really Trying*

We hear people throw around the phrase "donate my body to science" regularly, but what does it mean exactly? Basically, even if you were never smart enough for med school in life, you could end up there in death—and even contribute to amazing breakthroughs. (So, Dad, are you proud of me *now*?)

The medical uses for dead bodies make them sound extremely precious, almost magical. Imagine being a key part of training aspiring doctors, advancing surgical techniques, finding new treatments for cancer or diabetes or HIV, developing cutting-edge medical equipment, or helping people walk again through spinal injury research, to name just a few possibilities—all without lifting a finger. Even better, you can be an organ donor first and then donate the rest of you to science, saving lives not once but twice. In many cases, when a research institute is finished with your body, what remains of your remains will be cremated for free and the ashes returned to your family, ensuring you don't miss out on a burial. It's win-win-win for everyone.

Body donation is critical to medical science, and it's an extremely noble thing to do with your remains. But this is one area where you and your loved ones need to do some serious research. Bodies are worth a lot of money, and just like old-timey grave robbers, there are unscrupulous people looking to cash in. The horror stories that come out about smaller, unethical body brokers are too stomach-churning to get into.

*However*—this does not mean the whole business is bad, or that your remains will end up in a house of horrors only to be discovered when it's raided by police. There are many eminently respectable institutions that accept body donations, including the Mayo Clinic and Harvard Medical School. One of the ways you can tell if an organization is legit is that it will require a form signed by you while you're still alive. The person must make the body donation decision themselves, otherwise their family could be tempted by the money or funeral discounts that many shady brokers offer. So don't be scared off by the headlines, but do let them motivate you to thoroughly do your homework if you want to contribute to science after you're gone.

## BODY FARMS: *Or, Fun with Forensics*

Maybe you're not that into medical science, but you love anything true crime related. If *CSI* is more your thing, you can still donate your body after death. Wait till you get a load of this.

The first body farm was founded at the University of Tennessee in Knoxville in 1971. This is how it works: corpses (always from willing volunteers) are left outside on the "farm" in various environmental situations. That might mean buried in a shallow grave, submerged in a lake, or shut in the trunk of a car. Then nature takes its course, and researchers and students from law enforcement and forensic science disciplines study how the bodies decompose, what insects show up, and other icky but case-solving techniques you've seen on any number of crime shows. In real life, being able to prove timelines, locations, and more really does solve cases. Your body donation could keep an innocent person out of jail or send a murderer to prison. After a body has been reduced to bones, it is saved in a skeletal collection and continues to help with advances in body identification.

There are many similarities between donating your body to science and giving it to a body farm. You'll need to make the decision official while still alive and get signatures on the forms so everyone knows it's on the level. You can also be an organ donor before your body goes to the farm. And sometimes free services are on offer, such as transportation of your corpse if you happen to expire within one hundred miles of the University of Tennessee. (So if you are on a budget and start having chest pains, get there in a hurry.)

Body farms have extra rules, though. The Tennessee center, for instance, cannot accept bodies if the deceased contracted certain diseases, and it requires photos

# BECOMING POOR YORICK

If you're an actor or you've always dreamed of treading the boards, your death could be your big break. A starring role in *Hamlet* awaits you, and you don't have to memorize any lines. Critics might call your performance wooden, but really it will be more . . . bony.

There's a tradition of donating one's skull to be used as a prop in the famous scene where Hamlet exclaims, "Alas, poor Yorick! I knew him, Horatio: a fellow of infinite jest, of most excellent fancy." Poor Yorick is very dead, and his remains have just been uncovered by gravediggers. So Hamlet picks up his skull and talks to it, but Hamlet is going through some things, so it's forgivable.

The first recorded use of a human skull in a production of *Hamlet* was, strangely enough, by the actor father of John Wilkes Booth, who assassinated Abraham Lincoln. Allegedly, it was willed to him by an old cellmate who was hanged. Others have followed suit, the most famous being the Polish composer André Tchaikowsky, whose skull was used in a 2008 Royal Shakespeare Company production starring David Tennant as Hamlet.

Unfortunately, the legal and practical barriers to skull donation are numerous, so if treading the boards postmortem is for you, you can either fob it off on your survivors to hopefully figure out or lobby for permission while you're still alive. Also, be sure to warn the theater company you bequeath your dome to, because unexpectedly getting a skull in the mail screams mobster more than Shakespeare.

(for facial reconstruction research) as well as a detailed biological questionnaire from the donor. Because of the complexity of the process, the center recommends that you hire a lawyer. But once you are finally signed up, they give you a cool donor card to carry with you.

The other big difference is, while cadaver donation facilities are so common you can trip over them, there are only seven body farms in the U.S. and one in Australia. That's it. Starting a body farm is always controversial, and local residents often are afraid of seeing or smelling the bodies, or that they will attract vermin. However, Canada, India, and the United Kingdom have shown interest in starting their own farms, so if you live in one of those countries, keep an eye on updates and try to outlive the grindingly slow bureaucracy. But the current facilities are hardly overflowing. The University of Tennessee, for example, gets just one hundred bodies a year, so they'd be more than happy to have you.

## PLASTINATION: *You Could Be a Model*

Maybe you want your dead body to educate, but neither body donation nor body farms feel right. Maybe you're more artistic, more creative. Maybe you don't just want to die and decompose . . . you want to become art.

In that case, plastination is just the thing for you. If the Body Worlds exhibit has ever come to your area, you have probably heard of this process. People are often shocked by the anatomical displays. Indeed, what at first look like detailed models of the insides of humans actually *are* humans.

If you've never seen a plastinated body, imagine a life-size, skinless Barbie doll. The muscles, veins, and internal organs are visible. The body is posed mid-action, allowing viewers to learn how all those normally hidden bits work together. It's enlightening and provocative for regular people, but for medical students it's also a valuable educational tool. A 2013 article from the peer-reviewed *Journal of Anatomy* trumpeted the benefits of using plastinated tissue samples, which are perfect examples of the needed specimen that never degrade, never decompose, and can be used by class after class of future doctors and surgeons. The detail and durability of plastination is a huge boon to medical science.

But while the final product is eerily beautiful, the process of becoming plastinated is somehow even more stomach-churning than embalming. The Body Worlds website explains the five-step procedure, which includes stages like removing all your skin, 500 to 1,000 hours of dissection, and something called "forced impregnation" (which just refers to getting the plastic into your cells, but damn, that's a terrible name for it). The whole process takes about a year, after which your plasticky remains are used by medical schools or put on display in the exhibits for laypeople.

According to the Body Worlds website, as of 2019 almost 20,000 people had donated their corpses for plastination. The vast, vast majority (about 89 percent) were from Germany, which makes sense because that is where the process originated, but you can't help thinking it says something about the people there. If you want to join them one day, you'll need to get ahold of the Institute for Plastination in Heidelberg to start the official process.

# NINE NIGHTS

The Caribbean tradition of Nine Nights comes from the region's history of slavery and the intermingling of West African and Christian beliefs. It's believed that the spirit of the deceased (specifically the evil part, called the "duppy") can't leave the body until the ninth night after the person dies. If the duppy doesn't leave, it will stick around and cause misfortune. So to give it a proper send-off, mourners gather to feast, tell stories about the departed, and often party pretty hard. Customarily, this event lasts the full nine days and nights, although some modern Nine Nights only take place on the final evening.

On that ninth night, a religious figure will perform a ceremony meant to release the deceased's spirit. There may be an altar with offerings to keep the duppy happy, like flowers and rum. By tradition, the furniture in the house is rearranged to confuse the spirit and make it want to leave. Mirrors are covered to prevent future hauntings—not that you should let that stop you if your loved ones hold a Nine Night (see "Coming Back to Haunt Someone," page 162). It's important to keep the mood light, so people sing and play dominos and cards, and the night usually ends in dancing. The spirit of the deceased may possess a family member and pass on their last wishes through them.

In the morning, after a long and tiring night, the family will clean the house, throwing the used glasses into the street. They may also burn or give away the deceased's clothing and other possessions. But finally, if the ceremonies and offerings have worked, the spirit will move on, leaving for their ancestral African homeland.

# Traditional Methods

Perhaps surprisingly, a lot of the traditional ways our ancestors disposed of their dead are illegal today. Some of them are myths that never happened in the first place. But a few are still an option if you want to return to your roots (in more ways than one).

## MUMMIFICATION: *Still a Thing!*

For most people, the first thing that comes to mind when thinking about mummification is ancient Egypt. Even if you fell asleep that day in history class, Hollywood has made mummies and ancient Egypt synonymous. And for good reason: that civilization loved them some mummies. The first mummies might have been accidental, bodies simply dried out and preserved by the sand and heat of the region. But by 2600 BCE, Egyptians were making mummies on purpose. They did such a great job of it that today, thousands of years later, many of these mummies look as good as the day they were buried. Since preserving the body was important for religious reasons, many high-status and even some common Egyptians went through the process—not just famous pharaohs like King Tut.

And it was one hell of a process, taking seventy days from beginning to end. Since organs decompose faster, they were removed first and stored separately. The brain was removed through the nose with a special hook. The body was dried with salt, until all the moisture was gone. Just like with embalming today, the ancient Egyptians wanted their corpses to look lifelike, so they were filled with cloth to fatten them up again and given fake eyes. Hundreds of yards of linen completed the classic mummy look. And during all of this, the priest doing the job performed rituals and offered prayers.

While the Egyptians are the most famous for it, plenty of other civilizations have mummified their dead over the centuries. Not only that, it's still an option for you today! The modern religion of Summum, founded in 1975, practices mummification, and in 2008, its founder, Claude Nowell, was the first to undergo the 1,000-hour procedure. It wouldn't be as cool without a pyramid, though, so their headquarters in Salt Lake City has one, and that's where his remains were laid to rest. The group offers their mummification services to anyone—you don't have to subscribe to their belief system. They mummify pets and humans, but if you are considering it, start saving now. As of 2020, the process costs $67,000 for US residents, according to their website. Still, you'd be a mummy, and you can't put a price on how cool that is.

## VIKING SHIP SEND-OFF: *Going Out in a Blaze of Glory*

Hollywood has convinced us that Vikings sent their dead out to sea in a ship, whereupon an archer shot a flaming arrow and the mourners watched as the deceased was cremated in a totally badass display. Sadly, this probably wasn't a thing. The key problem is that a flaming arrow couldn't have generated enough heat to burn the body, so instead of majestically cremating their loved one, the Vikings would have instead gotten a charred corpse washed up on the beach in a few days, and no one wants that. However, some important Vikings were *buried* in their ships, often with tons of grave goods, including sacrificed slaves. Important burials were sometimes marked with standing stones that formed the outline of a ship. But there is a kernel of truth in the flaming fanta-sy, though; many Vikings were cremated on funeral pyres together with their grave goods.

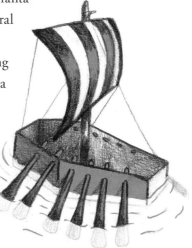

If your dream of going out in a flaming Viking funeral has just been crushed, fear not—there is a scaled-down modern way to do it. A U.K. company called Cradle to Grave makes a small, watertight willow model of a Viking ship, in which your loved ones can put some of your ashes before setting it ablaze. The boats are not only biodegradable, but fully customizable, too.

# TURNING BODY ART INTO FINE ART

Tattoos aren't called body art for nothing. These permanent markings can be beautiful, meaningful, and as much a personal identifier as someone's eyes or smile. You can get them done on the cheap (in prison, for example), or they can run into the thousands of dollars. Whatever the cost, it's a real shame that these masterpieces are lost when the person they belong to dies.

Fortunately, it doesn't have to be that way! Companies like Save My Ink Forever or the nonprofit National Association for the Preservation of Skin Art (NAPSA) will remove your tattoos (meaning, your epidermis) after death, preserve them, and mount them as framed artwork. The whole process takes about three months. Tattoos are divisive in life, and the act of preserving tattoos after death is even more so. But this option may appeal to people who take pride in their skin art.

Some tattoo enthusiasts hope that one day we'll all have the body art of our forbearers preserved and framed on our walls, just as people keep urns full of ashes on their mantels. At the very least, it would be a hell of a talking point. Maybe put Grandpa's naked lady tattoo in a closet before you bring a new date over, though. Until the practice becomes common, displaying human skin will just scream serial killer—and that really ruins the mood.

# WHAT TO DO with MY BODY

This is the big one. Everything else is window dressing. Important window dressing, which will affect how your loved ones remember saying goodbye to you for the rest of their lives, but still just icing on the funeral cake. (Are funeral cakes a thing? We need to make those a thing.)

You may be able to make some arrangements now, like reserving a spot on a rocket or starting the paperwork for body donation. Maybe you can even pay in advance, locking in today's prices. Make sure you look into the laws in your chosen location, to ensure that your wishes are legal and so you know what permits are needed (if any).

**DESCRIBE YOUR BODY DISPOSAL METHOD OF CHOICE:**

......................................................................................................................

......................................................................................................................

**DO ARRANGEMENTS NEED TO BE MADE IN ADVANCE? LIST THEM.**

......................................................................................................................

......................................................................................................................

......................................................................................................................

**ANY SPECIAL REQUESTS OR OTHER THINGS TO NOTE (E.G., WOULD YOU LIKE TO DONATE YOUR ORGANS, BE EMBALMED, ETC.)?**

......................................................................................................................

......................................................................................................................

......................................................................................................................

......................................................................................................................

# BUILD YOUR OWN COFFIN

**F**ormer palliative care nurse Katie Williams was sick of going to funerals that didn't feel personal. So she had a brilliant idea: a club where you could build and decorate your coffin before you died. That way, at least you would be buried in something that represents the real you. And if the real you is paintings of your cats or your favorite sports team's logo, so be it.

Instead of running screaming from the crazy person, the people of New Zealand embraced the concept. Williams started the first coffin club in 2010, and within a few years, four more had sprung up around the small country. Describing themselves as "makers of fine, affordable underground furniture" or designers of their "final bedrooms," the clubs are, ironically, keeping people alive. The comradery and personal connections help senior citizens combat loneliness and give them a new purpose.

If you're part of the 99.94 percent of the world's population that doesn't live in New Zealand, you can still make your own coffin. Woodworking plans are available online. Fred Guentert of Florida, for example, spent 25 years making a 300-pound Egyptian-style coffin for himself. And if you think having your coffin standing in the corner for a couple of decades is weird, Williams reminds us, "It's a box until there is someone in it."

# HOW to CONTAIN my REMAINS

If applicable, describe the container you would like your remains placed in (whether a coffin, urn, or something less conventional), as well as special requests or other things to note. For example, would you like guests to sign your coffin before it's interred? Do you already have the urn of your dreams waiting patiently in your garage? Or are you going with an unconventional burial container, like a mushroom suit or tree pod? If you are being laid to rest in a coffin or urn, draw your dream design on the templates provided below.

# You CAN Take It with You

Obviously, the most tragic part about dying is the people you will leave behind and the experiences you will miss out on. But you're not supposed to care about all your precious belongings getting chucked in a dumpster or, worse, being fought over by undeserving relatives. "You can't take it with you" is a maxim some of us pretend to agree with, while secretly wishing we could go out like pharaohs. Humans like our material possessions, and we don't necessarily want to be parted from them just because of the technicality of dying. Not much has changed since ancient Egypt, really, except it's much harder to get gold coffins now.*

Funerals are about so much more than just getting rid of a body. They are a complex social ritual that is almost uniquely human.** That may have all started with grave goods. About 100,000 years ago, early humans began burying their loved ones with *stuff*. Archaeologists can tell the difference between lovingly placed items and junk that was just thrown in a pit, so these burials are a clue to when *Homo sapiens* really became human.

In short, taking your possessions with you to the grave isn't selfish or materialistic—it's a fundamental act of being a person. And who knows, maybe our ancestors were right and you will need those things on the other side. Perhaps Charon really does charge to ferry you across the River Styx, and you'll need some cash. The ancient Egyptians would tell you to take plenty of food and drink for the journey. And lots of cultures were certain you would need some servants in the hereafter, so try to get your relatives to volunteer for the job. (Start working on that ASAP, because they will probably need some convincing.)

Let's take a minute to consider all the things you can refuse to be parted from, even in death.

---

\* Not impossible, though. The "Promethean," made famous by the corpses of both Michael Jackson and James Brown, is a $24,000 gleaming statement piece. Okay, technically, it's made of polished bronze, but it looks golden and the hardware is all 24-karat gold plated, so it counts.

\** Although elephants and chimpanzees have their own ways of honoring their dead, they have yet to build forty-story-tall pyramids when their leaders kick the bucket.

## TREASURES IN HEAVEN (and on Earth, Too)

We're talking things like Bibles, yarmulkes, and rosaries here, not religious ar-
tifacts in the sense of Indiana Jones–style relics stolen from a snake-filled crypt.
Although, if you do have a saint's shin bone or the Ark of the Covenant knocking
around, you might want to consider bringing it with you. Could be useful if you
need to bribe St. Peter.

If you haven't spent your life collecting splinters of the True Cross, there are still
plenty of meaningful religious objects that it would make sense to be buried or
cremated with. For people who follow some kind of spiritual belief system, religion
and death are inextricably linked. Whether you believe death leads to an afterlife
or reincarnation or nothing at all, it can be comforting to know you will have a
religious text or other paraphernalia along for the ride. Some religions have rules
about what can and can't be done with their holy books, so make sure you are
being respectful before you hedge your bets and request one of everything.

## DIAMONDS ARE FOREVER (Going to Be a Source of Conflict)

Perhaps the biggest decision to make when it comes to what to take with you into
death is jewelry. Unlike just about everything else you could choose, precious
metals can last almost forever, so jewelry can be passed down to many future
generations to appreciate. Jewelry also has a lot of sentimental value, so your loved
ones might not want to see it buried, burned, or sunk to the bottom of the ocean.
And, to state the obvious, some jewelry is worth serious coin. While your relatives
will be happy to bury you with all the worthless snack food and flowers you desire,
they might balk at a couple-carat engagement ring disappearing forever. All of
those are fair arguments, even the one that makes your next of kin sound like they
are out for what they can get. As much as you might be attached to your jewelry,
it's worth considering if those baubles would be better off with the living.

On the other hand (literally, if we're talking rings), if you wore a piece for years,
or at a particularly important moment of your life, it's perfectly understandable
to want not to be parted from it in death. And there's plenty of precedent. King

# HOW TO FEND OFF GRAVE ROBBERS

Graverobbers don't always skulk around under cover of darkness. Sometimes they show up bright and early—and with permits. If you decide to take so much stuff with you that your burial could be classified as a hoard, expect to be dug up and all your precious possessions to be moved to a museum in a few hundred years. Such was the case with the important ship burial at Sutton Hoo in England, where a tribal king or warrior was buried with elaborate and expensive weapons, armor, and an absolute fortune in gold decoration. And anyone of any importance buried in ancient Egypt has famously been raided by grave robbers and archaeologists alike over the millennia.

If you want to keep your stuff buried with you for eternity, consider the tactics of Qin Shi Huang, the first emperor of China, who died in 210 BCE. Ancient records indicate that his earthen mausoleum includes, among other things, "rivers of mercury." That's a big reason the tomb hasn't been excavated to reach the riches inside—if you tried, the results could be fatal. Yet archaeologists did manage to get their hands on his buried Terracotta Army. Learn from Qin's mistake: make sure you cover absolutely everything in your grave with rivers of mercury. No exceptions.

Tut was buried with so much jewelry, he's probably managing a Tiffany's in the Field of Reeds to this day. Tabloid reports that Whitney Houston was buried in $500,000 worth of diamonds sparked grave-robbing fears. So unless you're worried your loved ones will literally dig you up to get the shiny stuff back, feel free to take all of it with you.

## FOOD AND DRINK FOR THE JOURNEY: *Have Your Cake and Don't Eat It, Too*

The ancient Egyptians might have been right that the afterlife is BYOB, but even if they weren't, there are plenty of reasons you might want to bring some snacks with you anyway. Food is awesome. Sure, it's necessary for existence, but you don't see people requesting to be buried with broccoli. It's the yummy food, the comfort food, the food anyone would miss that people want slipped into their coffins and urns.

Which means you might want some booze for the ride. Honestly, you could stop there, because alcohol is all you will ever need, but if you are a teetotaler or not the type to drink on an empty stomach, the options are endless.

Take Leonard Durkin, who died at age seventy-one in 2019. In life, he used to order a Bacon Double Cheeseburger from Burger King to eat while visiting his

wife's grave. He asked his son to make sure he got to enjoy that meaningful fast food in death as well. But no one warned the staff at the Burger King in Leeds, England, so they were probably shocked when a hearse rolled up to their drive-through as the funeral cortege stopped to pick up Durkin's final order. The burger was lovingly placed on the coffin before they made their way to the crematorium.

## CELL PHONES: *Your Lifeblood, Even in Death*

Now that humans have essentially become androids, never without our smartphones in hand, you won't be surprised to learn that taking your cell to the grave has become common. We're obsessed with our phones, barely able to look up from them long enough to enjoy quality time with people who will miss us when we're gone. Why would you want to leave behind all your high scores in Candy Crush, filthy sext messages, and thousands of photos of your cat? This one small item fits easily in a coffin or urn and holds so much of your life within it.

But many people take this a step further. While you won't get service in a grave even if you find yourself unfortunately alive enough to answer a call (see "How to Avoid Being Buried Alive," page 21), mourners can find comfort in burying or interring the deceased with a phone and then keeping the service going. As long as someone continues paying the bill, loved ones can call the number and hear the deceased's voice, then leave a voicemail they can kind of imagine the deceased getting somehow. It's like sending a letter to heaven for the twenty-first century. Everyone knows it doesn't work like that, but in the middle of mourning, the happy fiction might allow people to feel closer to the person they lost.

# EVERYTHING BUT THE KITCHEN SINK

There's really no end to the list of things you can put in your coffin or urn, as long as they fit. According to Fioritto Funeral Service in Cleveland, Ohio, the following are the top ten items people are buried with.

- BOOKS: *Religious or otherwise, they get bonus points for not harming the environment.*

- PHOTOS: *Often complete with frames*

- TICKET STUBS/PROGRAMS

- STUFFED ANIMALS

- ALCOHOL/CIGARETTES *(Hey, you don't need to worry about them killing you anymore!)*

- SPORTS MEMENTOS

- CASH, JEWELRY, OR OTHER VALUABLES

- CREMATED REMAINS: *Especially of pets, although there are rules about this (see "Pet Cemeteries: The Not-Evil Kind," page 30)*

- ELECTRONIC DEVICES: *Vital, but definitely not good for the environment*

- FLOWERS

# CELEBRITY BURIAL HOARDS

If you're embarrassed to request to be buried with your favorite game console and/or rubber band ball, don't worry your pretty head. Plenty of people have been buried with way weirder items. Here is just a handful of the creative choices celebrities have made when it came to their grave goods.

## TONY CURTIS

After the actor died peacefully in his sleep in 2010, he was laid to rest in a casket that was so packed with stuff, it's amazing there was room for his body. Among the dozens of items were a model of his car, his navy medals, a pair of his grandson's baby shoes, stones he'd collected while traveling, a DVD of clips from his favorite films, his iPhone, seven packets of Splenda, a single Percocet tablet, and his dog's ashes. And more. Lots more. His widow listed all the things he was being buried with in his eulogy, because together, they explained the story of his life.

## FRANK SINATRA

The singer had a certain image while alive, and he carried his brand even into death. When he died in 1998, Sinatra's coffin contained a pack of Camel cigarettes, a Zippo lighter, and a bottle of his favorite tipple: Jack Daniel's whiskey. The spirits company even mentioned that Old Blue Eyes took their product to the grave in a TV commercial. He was also buried with ten dimes, so he would always be able to call his friends. (See, before cell phones, we had to use something called a "pay phone" and . . . actually, just ask your grandparents.)

## BOB MARLEY

The iconic reggae musician was only thirty-six when he died of cancer in 1981. It probably goes without saying that he couldn't go to his grave without his red Gibson Les Paul guitar. His Rastafarian religion was represented through his grave goods as well, with a Bible opened to Psalm 23 ("The Lord is my shepherd") and a stalk of marijuana, placed on his chest by his widow, Rita Marley.

## WILLIAM S. BURROUGHS

The writer died in 1997 and was reportedly buried with items including a fedora, a joint, and a sword cane (is there any cooler item to be buried with?). Burroughs also took a loaded .38-caliber revolver with him, which is odd enough on its own but even more unsettling when you learn that he accidentally shot and killed his second wife while drunk in 1951.

## ARCH WEST

The inventor of Doritos proved that just because you're being cremated doesn't mean you can't take some fun stuff with you. Before interring his urn in 2011, friends and family tossed Doritos into the burial box. West didn't actually request this, but his daughter said he would think it was "hilarious."

## SANDRA WEST

No relation to Arch of Doritos fame, this West was a socialite used to the finer things in life, and her death in 1977 was not going to change that. She was dressed in lingerie and laid to rest in her powder-blue 1964 Ferrari 330 America. The grave was 19 feet long, 10 feet wide, and 9 feet deep, and it took a crane to lower the car and Mrs. West in there. It was one heck of an expensive coffin, and to thwart anyone who might attempt the most bizarre and time-consuming carjacking of all time, the whole thing was encased in concrete.

# My BURIAL ACCESSORIES

When deciding which items you want to be buried or cremated with, consider questions such as: Will they fit in your coffin? Can they be cremated, or do they need to be put in your urn afterward? Will taking an heirloom with you cause years of family squabbles? Does causing a family squabble sound fun, and will it ensure that you'll be remembered for generations to come? Where in the coffin or on your body do you want the items placed? (For example, Harry Houdini's pillow was a stack of letters from his mother, and George Burns had three cigars in his breast pocket.)

Express your wishes below—and remember to include combinations to safes, locations of keys, etc., in the "current location" section. Going through a deceased loved one's possessions can be a long, bittersweet, and painful process. The last thing your next of kin needs is to be ripping apart your closet looking for your signed DVD copy of *Paul Blart: Mall Cop* an hour before your burial.

ITEM:_____

DESCRIPTION:_____

PLACEMENT (ON BODY):_____

CURRENT LOCATION:_____

SENTIMENTAL VALUE:_____

ITEM:_____

DESCRIPTION:_____

PLACEMENT (ON BODY):_____

CURRENT LOCATION:_____

SENTIMENTAL VALUE:_____

ITEM:_____

DESCRIPTION:_____

PLACEMENT (ON BODY):_____

CURRENT LOCATION:_____

SENTIMENTAL VALUE:_____

# WHAT TO WEAR WHEN YOU'RE DEAD

It's not just what you're buried *with*, but what you are buried *in*. Your final outfit is just as important as your grave goods, especially if you are having an open casket funeral or a family-involved cremation where everyone will see you looking fabulous one last time.

If you've spent the years developing a signature style, don't give it up right at the end. Plenty of people went out in their most famous threads, like Bela Lugosi, who wore a replica of the cape from his *Dracula* films. Or Kentucky Fried Chicken's Harland Sanders, the Colonel himself, who was buried in his famous white suit and black string bow tie. You might not have defined your style brand so acutely, but there's no reason not to exit this life looking distinctly yourself—and it's never too late to start wearing leopard print or feather boas!

# My FINAL FASHION STATEMENT

Your final send-off will likely involve one last choice of outfit. (If you're not into fashion, perhaps consider a naked option, like plastination; see page 45.) This is the last thing you will ever wear, your last chance to look good. Fashion is political, it's personal, and it's hard to get right. This will take some real thought.

What garments are meaningful to you? What is most flattering? (It's not easy to make a corpse look fabulous, so don't make it any harder on the funeral directors. If you can't squeeze into those jeans that made your butt look great when you were twenty-two, accept it and move on.) Pick whatever you love, even if it's a bit unconventional. Who says you can't go out in your wedding dress or favorite Speedo?

Use the space below to describe the outfit you'd like to exit this life in, then sketch it on the figure provided. Be sure to include shoes, hats, or jewelry.

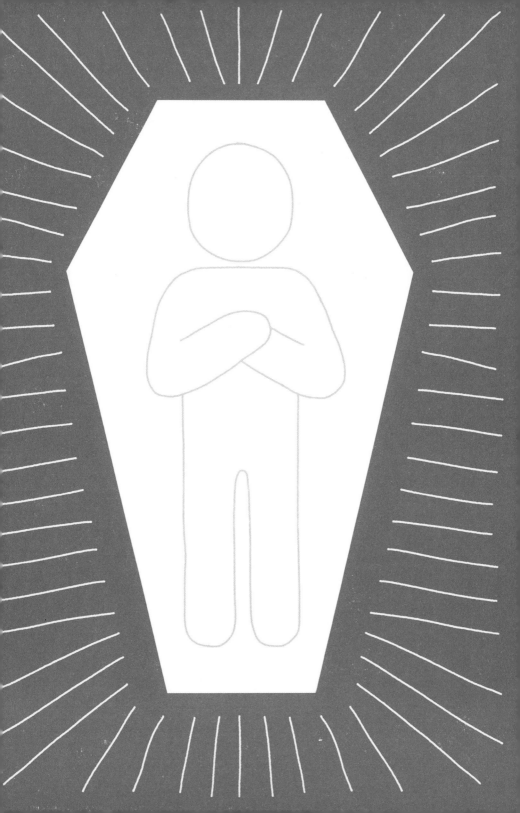

# WHAT CAN BE CREMATED WITH ME?

When someone is given a standard burial, taking everything they want with them in the coffin isn't an issue. (Except those pesky still-alive servants. People frown on that nowadays.) But if you choose cremation and that coffin crammed with stuff is set on fire, suddenly you have to worry about annoying details like "explosions" and "burning down the crematory."

That means you can't be cremated with a cell phone, a bottle of alcohol (buzzkill), and anything made of vinyl, treated leather, or latex (so your wish to go out in your gimp suit is never going to be granted . . . for many reasons). Pacemakers must be removed from the body as well. Only flammable coffins can be cremated, and many crematories don't allow any items in the furnace at all.

So be sure to check with your local crematory ahead of time, or invest in a larger urn so you can fill it with all the uncremated booze and condoms you want for the ultimate afterlife party.

# WAKES

A wake is a social gathering, typically held before the funeral and with the body present. The word *wake* refers to the ancient tradition of keeping watch over a body before burial, which goes back at least to the pre-Christian Celtic countries of Europe and their pagan religions. It most likely stemmed from the belief that an evil spirit could possess the corpse before burial if one wasn't vigilant, and as Hollywood has made abundantly clear, zombies are less than ideal. After Christianity largely replaced ancient beliefs in Celtic Europe, wakes still stuck around, but prayers were added and the possession angle was downplayed.

But no matter which religion was in charge, the European wake was all about getting drunk. The corpse was placed under a table (with a plate of salt on its chest, for reasons that probably made sense at the time) and the table was then loaded down with alcohol. Sometimes there was also a feast, because not everyone can handle "drinking orgies" (as the *Encyclopedia Britannica* calls these early wakes) on an empty stomach.

Wakes haven't changed much, minus the salt and the body's proximity to the booze. Modern wakes are still about celebrating the deceased in a more relaxed atmosphere, where people eat and drink away their sorrows. Having the dead person present is optional now, although many people still choose to include them. While some people hold serious, mournful vigils that are all about somberly remembering the deceased, there's something wonderful about the original style of wake (okay, yes, I mean the booze) and the happiness it involved. Consider insisting your family follow this tradition to a T. They'll probably thank you for it (or they would, if you weren't dead).

# PART TWO

# IT'S YOUR Funeral

# IT'S YOUR FUNERAL
## AND YOU CAN DIE IF YOU WANT TO

Funerals haven't always been the cookie-cutter events they often are today. Since everyone who has ever lived has also died, each generation and civilization has put their own stamp on the proceedings. Funerals have gone through fads and fashions, just like all human milestones.

To past generations, many things we now do routinely at funerals would seem offensive, dangerous, uncaring, overly dramatic, or not dramatic enough. But even today, different religions, cultures, and individuals have wildly different ideas about the correct way to lay someone to rest. That's why planning your funeral is so important—because death and mourning are deeply personal, and what seems logical and meaningful even to those closest to you might in no way correspond to your expectations. You can't please everyone, so just worry about pleasing the most important person at the funeral: you.

The point is, there's no right way to have a funeral. When it comes to all the planning considerations in this chapter—from the venue, dress code, and decorations to the readings, music, and interment style—follow your bliss, even if your bliss is unconventional. You won't be around to see your stuffy cousins rolling their eyes, so what's stopping you?

# Funeral Traditions of Major Religions

For many people, funerals are inextricably tied to religion. When your spiritual beliefs hold that death is a major step into something new, be it reincarnation, some kind of afterlife, or other ethereal realms, of course your funeral is going to be a big deal. It involves your loved ones recognizing that step and saying good-bye to the person you were, while also sending you off on your spiritual journey. Even people who aren't religious may find comfort in some of the traditions that different faiths have developed around death. If you follow one of these religions and want to have your funeral service in a house of worship, here are some of the rituals you might be expected to abide by.

Please note: This is a very brief overview of these religious traditions, so don't take it as, well, gospel. Also remember that religious sects have variations and may do things differently.

## CHRISTIANITY

For many people in the West, the Christian rite is what springs to mind when we think about funerals. It's what we mostly see portrayed on-screen, and it more or less follows the Victorian template. The funeral takes place in a church and includes prayers, hymns, scripture readings, and a eulogy. After the service, the remains are taken to the graveyard or cemetery (or, increasingly, to a columbarium or urn garden, since most Christian denominations are fine with cremation). There the priest or minister reads the committal service, which traditionally includes the famous line, "We therefore commit this body to the ground; earth to earth, ashes to ashes, dust to dust."

## ISLAM

A basic tenet of Muslim funerals is that they happen quickly, usually within twenty-four hours of death. When a person dies, family members wash the body and cover it with a shroud before transporting the corpse to the funeral site. The body is almost always in a coffin, because cremation is not allowed (embalming and autopsies are also discouraged). An imam leads the funeral prayers while mourners face in the direction of the holy city of Mecca. The body is then transported to the cemetery for burial, which traditionally excludes women and children. Each man present at the graveside throws three handfuls of dirt onto the coffin. A period of mourning follows.

## JUDAISM

It's preferred that a funeral take place within twenty-four hours of death, although it cannot be held on Shabbat or Jewish holidays. Attending is considered important, even if one has to travel far, because comforting mourners and accompanying another Jewish person to their grave are considered *mitzvot* (commandments). Close family members have a special status as *avelim*, or official mourners, who have religious traditions and rituals they are supposed to follow. Before the funeral service begins, avelim tear fabric (either a ribbon they are given or their clothes) to symbolize a physical manifestation of their grief. Prayers are recited during the service and at the graveside. Ideally, a Jewish person's coffin should be simple and completely biodegradable, with no nails, and embalming is discouraged. Mourners throw earth on the coffin, including some from Israel if possible. Then the family returns home to start a week of shiva, a period of structured mourning during which the focus is on reflection and outsiders coming to comfort the avelim.

## HINDUISM

Hindu funerals have three parts. First is the funeral service, often at home, led by a Hindu priest. Mourners wear white. Then the body is brought to the crematory (some Hindu sects practice burial, but cremation is most common). Traditionally, Hindus are cremated in pyres by the Ganges River, but any crematory is acceptable. At the cremation ceremony, the eldest son of the deceased presides, with guidance from a priest. Cremains are immersed, traditionally in the Ganges or another flowing body of water. Then the family enters a period of mourning, usually eleven to thirty-one days, until the *shraddha* ceremony. Led by the eldest son again, this rite is performed to honor the deceased and assist them in the spiritual realms before they are reincarnated.

# SHEMIRA

Judaism is an ancient religion, so it makes sense that this custom began due to issues that many people no longer have to deal with. Long before morgues or funeral homes, a deceased person would be kept in their home prior to burial, and their body could attract rats. Practicing *shemira*, or keeping watch over the deceased, ensured the body remained unmolested and respected until going to its final resting place.

According to the Talmud, the soul hangs around its old body for several days after death, feeling lost and confused in the transition period between life and burial. Those sitting shemira (the *shomrim*) often pray or read aloud from religious texts, especially Psalms or the Book of Job, which comforts the lingering soul as well as the shomrim.

Shomrim are not allowed to eat, drink, or smoke in the room with the body, out of respect for the spirit of the deceased, who can't enjoy doing those things anymore. More than one person can sit shemira, but someone must be with the body the whole time. Although many will volunteer to help the deceased's family in their time of need, it's considered acceptable to pay people to take a shift as well.

# FUNERALS FOR THE LIVING

**D**eath does not always come suddenly. Many of us see it approaching like a freight train, albeit one that's going to hit us in months or years. If you are diagnosed with a terminal disease, or have hit your ninth or tenth decade, you may want to consider having your funeral *before* you die.* It may sound counterintuitive, but living funerals are becoming more common. And people who have attended one almost unanimously say they are beautiful, moving events.

Consider that you're putting all this time (and money) into an event celebrating you, and then you won't even be there to experience it (on a mental and emotional level; physically, you'll probably be there). If you know the end is coming, with a more concrete timeline than the vague "the end is coming" we all face, why not schedule your funeral just a bit earlier so that when people say nice things about you, you can enjoy it?

It should be noted that living funerals are events where *everyone* knows that the person is alive and present. We are not talking about the soap opera cliché of faking your death and then attending your funeral to hear what everyone says about you and finally prove that your nemesis has been having an affair with your spouse (see "My Guest List and Pest List," page 112). Although that too is an option, and it sounds awesome.

---

\* Technically, there's no reason you can't throw yourself a living funeral even if you are young and healthy. It's not common, but fewer Millennials and Gen Zers are getting married, so there's definitely an opening for a new kind of celebration in your twenties or thirties!

## BUDDHISM

In keeping with the widespread perception that Buddhists are totally chill, there are no official Buddhist funeral guidelines. A Buddhist monk may lead the funeral, which can take place anywhere but is usually at a funeral home or Buddhist temple. There is often an altar with a large portrait of the deceased, candles, an image of Buddha, and offerings of flowers and fruit. Mourners may wear black or white, but not red, which is the color of celebration in many parts of Asia. Although most Buddhists are cremated, other choices of body disposal are fine as well. Whatever it is, it usually happens directly after the funeral service.

## WICCA

The first part of a Wiccan funeral involves laying the body on an altar. A priestess prepares the space and recites a ritual chant, which may be Celtic, pagan, or Wiccan. The priest and priestess will perform another recitation before mourners come forward to speak to the deceased and help them on their journey to the Summerland, the Wiccan afterlife, often described as an idyllic meadow. Then follows the burial of the body (or sometimes cremains). Because of Wiccan beliefs about respecting the earth and its life cycles, these funerals tend to be environmentally friendly, and natural burial is considered ideal. Wiccan funerals are often held outdoors in beautiful natural settings.

## ZOROASTRIANISM

Some adherents of this faith, which is practiced mainly in India, dispose of their dead in purpose-built circular stone structures called *dakhmas*, or towers of silence. It is believed that dead bodies are unclean and that cremation or burial can pollute the elements of earth and fire, which are held sacred. The flat roof of the dakhma has three concentric circles, one each for men, women, and children. Bodies are fed on by carrion birds and exposed to the elements, and after about a year, the dried bones are dropped into the pit in the center of the tower, where lime assists with their disintegration. Towers of silence are becoming less common, in part due to dwindling numbers of vultures in India, and in part because residents who live in the high-rises overlooking them complain about the view of decomposing bodies.

## SECULARISM/NO RELIGION

The number of people who follow no faith may be increasing rapidly, but mourners are still mourners, and rituals around death are still comforting to some. Secular, atheist, and humanist funerals have complete flexibility but often borrow from religious tradition, with their own spin. For example, instead of prayers, there might be speeches about the deceased; instead of scripture, there might be a reading from a book the deceased loved; instead of hymns, there may be secular songs. Secular funerals often put the focus on celebrating the person's life rather than mourning their death, and there are no constraints surrounding what happens to the body or when.

# FUNERAL CRASHERS

No, this is not just a joke in the 2005 film *Wedding Crashers*. There are people who really do show up at funerals for those they don't know, eat the food, chat with the mourners, and (probably) take a selfie with the corpse. Their reasons remain unclear, but you may want to plan for them. Once word gets out that you have planned yourself an amazing funeral, the metaphorical vultures will descend.[*]

In 2008, the English writer and broadcaster Victoria Coren was organizing her father's memorial service when she received an email warning her about the Jolley Gang. Led by ringleader Terence Jolley, this group apparently devoted their morbid social lives to gaining admittance to strangers' funeral and memorial services. Coren discovered that members of the group had indeed contacted her, claiming they knew her father and wanted invites. She confirmed her suspicions by placing an announcement in the paper for a memorial for the fictitious "Sir William Ormerod." Within hours, she had emails from all the same individuals, claiming they'd known and cherished dear Sir William and that they would love to attend.

In the end, Coren decided it was more trouble than it was worth to keep the Jolley Gang from attending her father's memorial ceremony. And attend they did. One forgot the fake name she'd given and had to be reminded of it by an usher. Mostly they were quiet, but they noshed plenty of food.

So, be warned. Word of your meticulously planned funeral will surely get out. Either tell your family it's a "the more the merrier" event, or budget for security.

---

[*]  If literal vultures descend, you may be having a Zoroastrian burial (see "Zoroastrianism," page 75).

# Choosing the Perfect Venue

When most people think of a funeral venue, they picture a house of worship or a VFW hall or a funeral home. While these locations may seem boring, that might actually be a positive for the still-alive people who will be attending. Since death is so jarring and scary, presenting mourners with an experience they expect can help calm them. Sure, you can request that your funeral be held at your favorite strip club, hot-yoga studio, or mountaintop, but it would also be nice to consider a location that won't give some attendees a heart attack.

With that in mind, here are some of the most common places to hold funerals, memorials, receptions, and other end-of-life celebrations.

- HOUSE OF WORSHIP *(even if you're not religious, some faith groups, like Unitarian Universalists, will host secular funerals)*

- FUNERAL HOME OR CREMATORY

- COMMUNITY CENTER

- PUBLIC PARK OR BEACH

- YOUR HOME *(or the home of a family member)*

- BANQUET HALL

- HOTEL EVENT ROOM

- WEDDING VENUE *(during the off-season you can get good rates!)*

- A PLACE THAT WAS PARTICULARLY IMPORTANT TO YOU IN LIFE *(but maybe think long and hard if that place is a strip club)*

As with any event, you need to double-check that the location can accommodate the number of mourners you expect, that there's enough parking, and that you have the budget for it. If you're being buried in a coffin, make sure the venue has accessible routes to get it in and out, because while that could make for a fabulous mishap in a sitcom, your family probably just wants this event to go smoothly. If your burial or interment must occur shortly before or after the funeral service, you'll need to choose a location close to your final resting place. If you select somewhere more public, consider that passersby will ogle the funeral, since that's human nature. If you want your mourners to have more privacy in one of these spaces, see about setting up screens or tents.

Even if a venue seems open for everyone's use (like a park, for example), always check to make sure you're allowed to host a funeral there. One, so that your send-off won't run into scheduling conflicts, but more important, so that your loved ones won't find themselves getting kicked out because there's a dead body and they don't have the right permissions or permits. Even venues that seem perfect for a funeral might actually be squeamish about anything connected with death and not want to host one. (People are weird that way. They need to read this book, basically.)

There's also a big difference between the places you can host a funeral where there's going to be a corpse or cremains and the places you can hold a service with no body present. If you're planning a memorial or reception where *everyone* attending will be alive, your options expand to anywhere you could hold any other function: restaurants, historic buildings, private clubs, and so on.

## FUNERAL VENUES WITH A BIT MORE "LIFE"

Maybe you're not looking for normal. Sure, an unconventional venue might shock your mourners, but they can deal with it. It's your funeral, after all, and you won't be around for the fallout, so it's really about what makes *you* comfortable. Here are some unusual funeral venue options.

- MOVIE THEATER

- BOWLING ALLEY

- BREWERY, PUB, OR WINERY

- CRUISE SHIP

- MUSEUM

- ZOO

- GOLF COURSE

Some of these places might be okay with a memorial or urn viewing, but could blanch if there's a body involved. Others might be more open-minded. For example, the pub. In Ireland, pubs doubled as morgues starting in the mid-1800s, when the Potato Famine meant there were more bodies than mortuaries could handle. Since pubs had cold-storage areas for beer, they were the next best place to store a body. Publicans ran with it, and many became undertakers on the side, hosting funerals and wakes in their establishments. The tradition continued for decades, and while it's rare now, Irish pubs do host funerals from time to time. About 100 publicans in the country are still undertakers. And the tradition isn't limited to the Emerald Isle. A 2012 funeral for a Zimbabwean woman was held at her favorite drinking hole. Two years later, a Detroit bar hosted the funeral of an employee who'd worked there for twenty-five years.

If you can't find the perfectly weird, perfectly "you" venue that will accommodate your mourners, there are also funeral homes looking to change the game. For example, Hodges Funeral Home in Florida installed a wine cellar in 2014. Some have added dance floors. As people tire of the stodgy old funeral service—and more people choose cremation, which drastically increases the number of venues where a funeral can be held—funeral homes are adapting to survive. That means you're likely to find one locally that offers something a little different.

# My FUNERAL VENUE

Use the space below to name or describe your dream funeral venue.

What logistics need to be considered to make this dream funeral location a reality? For example, will your loved ones need to transport your body in a plane? Are permits required? Write down any important considerations that need to be taken in order to ensure your send-off happens at the perfect place.

Finally, if your first location doesn't work out, because by the time you die the venue has closed or was destroyed in an alien invasion, what's plan B?

# Assigning Funeral Roles

Enlisting your friends and family to participate in your funeral service is a great way to make your big day more personal and give your loved ones some agency over the event. Ultimately, that may help them feel useful and maybe even pleasantly distracted from the gaping chasm that your loss leaves in their lives.

If you have tons of folks you'd like to include in the service, that's great—there are plenty of jobs to go around. Some traditional funeral roles include eulogist, musician, singer, reader, obituary writer, and usher. But it's *your* big day—dream up as many jobs as you desire. If you want to have a flower girl lead your coffin down the aisle prior to your eternal union with death, I'm not going to stop you.

Two roles require serious consideration: the officiant and the pallbearers. The officiant is one of the biggest jobs there is, so be sure whomever you pick is up for it.* The person will need to remain emotionally stable throughout the event, and they should probably have an organizational mind as well as a talent for public speaking. (This is a difficult trifecta to find, so be on the lookout for new people to befriend who could nail this role when the time comes.) Don't give the role to someone who might be overwhelmed by the responsibility. It's kinder to them, plus you are trying to pull off the perfect funeral here, and your officiant having a breakdown five minutes in will make it that much more difficult.

If you're going out in a coffin, you're going to need pallbearers. Consider people who are strong and of similar height. They will need to be able to carry your coffin on their shoulders or at their waist, depending on your preference. You'll need six to eight pallbearers, depending on how heavy your coffin is. You can also select additional individuals to serve as honorary pallbearers who will follow the coffin but don't need to do the heavy lifting. (If you're being cremated, you can create a similar role for a person who carries the urn.)

There's no one right way to pick pallbearers; some cultures prefer they be non-relatives, whereas others choose from the individuals closest to the deceased, especially family. Members of fraternities or societies like the Masons often select other

---

* If you have your funeral in a house of worship, you may not have much choice. It may be expected that the resident head holy person will officiate. At least you'll know they won't get stage fright.

members for the job. Buddhist tradition expects pallbearers to eat a vegetarian diet and avoid alcohol for forty-nine days following the person's death.

Alternately, you can hire people to do the job, which isn't a bad idea if you want to be sure to avoid mishaps. In Ghana, a group of professional pallbearers has become famous for adding choreography to their coffin-carrying duties. (Though it's an impressive sight and something you could definitely consider for your own funeral, know that one of the most famous videos of the Dancing Pallbearers is of them dropping the coffin mid-act.) But even if dancing is too risky for your taste, perhaps there are other things your pallbearers could do to make your funeral more meaningful, such as wearing coordinated outfits or singing as they carry your coffin.

# My FUNERAL DREAM TEAM

Use this worksheet to assign the important roles at your funeral. Common jobs that need filling include the officiant, pallbearers, eulogist, musicians and/or singers, readers, obituary writer, and ushers, but it all depends on the needs of your dream funeral and the people you'd like to be involved. You can assign these roles to friends, family, professionals, or dream celebrity guests. Describe why you have chosen each person for their assignment.

I WOULD LIKE _____ TO BE MY _____

BECAUSE _____.

I WOULD LIKE _____ TO BE MY _____

BECAUSE _____.

I WOULD LIKE _____ TO BE MY _____

BECAUSE _____.

I WOULD LIKE _____ TO BE MY _____

BECAUSE _____.

I WOULD LIKE _____ TO BE MY _____

BECAUSE _____.

I WOULD LIKE _____ TO BE MY _____

BECAUSE _____.

I WOULD LIKE _____ TO BE MY _____

BECAUSE _____.

# Funeral Themes

The theme for most funerals is basically just "grief." And for good reason, since everyone attending is usually pretty darn sad. But that's no fun! Some funerals are billed as celebrations of life—for which guests are told not to wear black, for example—but that's not much of a theme either. We select themes for birthdays and weddings, so why not funerals as well?

This isn't a new idea. In 1875, the *Albany Register* reported on the odd will of a man in the Netherlands who was known as the "king of smokers" among his friends. The article claims he told his lawyer to invite all the smokers in the country to his funeral, where they would be gifted ten pounds of tobacco and specially carved commemorative pipes. Everyone was to smoke throughout the service and then dump the ash on the coffin. Given the time period, you have to question the story, but it's a great idea for your own funeral if you also, as the headline put it, "smoked 10 tons of tobacco and died."

If you insist on a more recent example with video evidence, Dallas's Golden Gate Funeral Home laid a Texas man to rest with a Christmas-themed funeral in 2012. It was broadcast on the very short-lived TLC reality show *Best Funeral Ever* (which will obviously need to be rebooted to show off the event you're planning).

Other themed funerals they showcased revolved around bowling, breakfast, the Olympics, candy, Hollywood, horror (which you have to admit is on point), game shows, the Wild West, boxing, Hawaii, and country music. There was even a wedding-themed funeral.

Maybe you're obsessed with some aspect of pop culture, like Harry Potter or Pokémon or K-pop. You could theme your send-off around dogs or cats, a band, a type of booze, your career; anything that feels special and personal is fair game.

The theme might be expressed as simply as your choice of funeral music or a dress code for guests. And what about you? Could you be dressed as James Bond in your coffin, martini glass and all? Even your coffin or urn can be part of the theme. (You'd be hard pressed to come up with a theme for which the perfect urn isn't readily available. For example, a Google search for "Star Trek urns" yields two million results and counting.) But you can go so much further. Ask your loved ones to decorate with themed balloons, bunting, or posters, serve themed food, give out themed gift bags—the opportunities are endless.

It might seem silly, but a theme is a great way to make the commemoration of your death more representative of who you were in life. It can also give the event a less formal, rigidly sad air. With the right theme, your send-off can be something your mourners will remember and talk about fondly for the rest of their lives.

# Fashioning Your Funeral

Your funeral is, above all, an event. It's the perfect event, really, because you can organize everything exactly how you want and never get stressed out on the day of. It's a party planner's dream (minus the fact that you won't be paid). Death offers few silver linings, so take advantage of them when you can.

Think of your funeral as an extravaganza where you are not just the party planner and star, but the stylist, decorator, and DJ. The entire occasion revolves around you, not just in the literal sense of your corpse/ashes/fireworks display, but also, more important, figuratively. At the center is the *essence* of you. Who you were, how you want to be remembered, and the manner in which you want people to celebrate and/or grieve are expressed by the choices you make. Here are some elements to consider:

## FLOWERS

It's always nice to ask mourners to donate to charity rather than send flowers for your funeral. It helps the needy, it makes you look like a wonderful person one last time, and it means that you control the selection of flowers. There's a "language" of flowers, one almost everyone is unaware of today but that was common knowledge for centuries. Consider the message you can secretly send with some of your funereal floral choices, according to the Flower Expert:

- **YELLOW CARNATION:** *Disdain or disappointment. You are, of course, disappointed you are dead.*

- **YELLOW HYACINTH:** *Jealousy. You are jealous of all the people who are still alive.*

- **PURPLE HYACINTH:** *Sorrow. Everyone better be experiencing this feeling at your funeral.*

- **DEEP DARK ROSE:** *Mourning. For the void you've left behind.*

- **A SINGLE DAFFODIL:** *Misfortune. Everyone at your funeral will also die one day, so don't get too comfortable, jerks!*

# DRESS CODE

Should attendees wear black or colors?

Black can be cliché, but it can also send a statement. You are gone; therefore, so is all color and light from the world. Black is slimming, so mourners will look good in pictures, thus making them more likely to post on Instagram. The palette might be muted, but everyone will match. It's hard to screw up all black. On the other hand, colors add to a party vibe. After all, Día de los Muertos would have an entirely different feel without the bright palette.

Should attendees dress comfortably or to the nines?

There are not often events where dressing up in fabulous formalwear is acceptable, so asking your guests to go all out marks your funeral as particularly important. But don't be afraid to set a casual dress code. The more casual the better. By asking your mourners to wear sweatpants, you are saying to them, "I am beyond pain now, as are you in that cotton fleece. Also, you're probably so sad I'm dead that you can't even pull yourself together enough to put on a belt. I get it. I truly was that awesome." Plus, a casual dress code could guarantee you are the best dressed person there, even if you do need assistance putting your outfit on.

# FOOD

Mourning is hungry work. In most cultures, there's an expectation that the people who show up to remember you will at least get some good grub in return. Here are traditional funeral foods from various countries and religions:

- **INDIA**: *fruit and samosas*

- **MORMONISM**: *funeral potatoes, a cheesy hash brown casserole*

- **JUDAISM**: *hard-boiled eggs or hamine eggs, which are cooked for up to 18 hours*

- **SOUTH KOREA**: *yukgaejang, a spicy beef soup*

- **IRELAND**: *wake cakes, made with cream cheese and fruit*

But there's no need to confine yourself to tradition. Your funeral food can express a theme, represent your favorite dishes, or be catered by your favorite restaurant.

## ACTIVITIES

There are plenty of ways to get your mourners involved in your funeral beyond just sitting there and crying. Some meaningful activities include:

- Invite guests to **SIGN YOUR CASKET**, like the ultimate senior yearbook.

- If you're being buried, guests can **BRING THEIR OWN SHOVELS** and each drop a shovelful of dirt into your grave.

- Have guests **DECORATE YOUR CASKET**, like one would a car after a wedding, but with 100% fewer condom balloons.

- **GIVE A SMALL FAVOR** to each guest, like a copy of your favorite book or a packet of seeds to plant. They'll be reminded of you every time they look at the favor.

- Guests can **PLACE AN OBJECT** that reflects their relationship with you in the coffin, urn, or grave.

- Since everyone will be flooded with memories, it's the perfect time to set up a **MEMORY BOARD** for mourners to fill with their happy recollections of you, like photos, notes, or ticket stubs from concerts you went to together.

> "You can't choreograph death, but you
> can choreograph your funeral."
>
> —MARINA ABRAMOVIĆ, PERFORMANCE ARTIST

# My FUNERAL DESIGN

Use this space to describe three ideas to help spice up your funeral, whether they be a theme, a decoration, an activity, a dress code, or a themed menu.

1. .................................................................................................................
   .................................................................................................................
   .................................................................................................................
   .................................................................................................................

2. .................................................................................................................
   .................................................................................................................
   .................................................................................................................
   .................................................................................................................

3. .................................................................................................................
   .................................................................................................................
   .................................................................................................................
   .................................................................................................................

# The Eulogy

The eulogy is a speech meant to revere and honor the deceased. Since that's you, in this case, the eulogy is obviously all-important. Assume that all those funeral crashers who will show up because they hear your funeral is going to be the event of a lifetime won't know you well (see "Funeral Crashers," page 77); the eulogy is their chance to understand who you were. They might be so touched they start crying, in which case your family could save some cash by sending the paid mourners home early (see "Rent-a-Mourner," page 106). For those who *do* know you, the eulogy can help put into words the complicated emotions they are feeling. Hearing someone else describe how special you were and verbalize their grief can assist others with the mourning process.

The eulogy does not have to be—and in many cases isn't—given by a close family member. The funeral might be too painful for your nearest and dearest, and getting up and talking about you could cause them to break down. What good is a speech full of anecdotes about how amazing you were if no one can understand it because of all the wailing? For that reason, a friend or officiant is a perfectly acceptable choice to give your eulogy.

Although there is no official structure for a eulogy, you might want to let your chosen eulogist know that it's best to keep anecdotes in chronological order, stay respectful (but funny is fine!), and be sure not to rush. If the person needs help organizing their many endearing thoughts about your beautiful existence, share this basic outline.

1.  Opening remarks ("Hi, I'm so-and-so. This is the deceased. Hi, deceased. Sorry you're dead," etc.)

2.  Thank everyone for coming, especially if they traveled a long way.

3.  If you choose a friend or distant relative to give your eulogy, they should offer condolences to those who were closer to you (your spouse, family, etc.). This is a good place to mention the special relationships you had with them.

4.  The main bit: Talk about the deceased (you) and just spread on the praise and compliments so very thick.

5. Some personal anecdotes about you. They might want to highlight your personality, strength of character, and important values or political leanings.

6. If you're religious, they should mention how good you were at being religious, whether it's true or not.

7. Wrap it up with some comforting words. Thank everyone again. Drop the mic. Get out of there.

Important note for Catholics, Episcopalians, and Anglicans: eulogies are technically verboten at funerals. The idea is that the church service is the most important thing, and a eulogy would distract from it. These rules apply only to the service, so if you want to remain a good Christian but also want a glowing eulogy, plan to have the speech given at the graveside or scattering ceremony or reception.

"A funeral eulogy is a belated plea for the defense delivered after the evidence is all in."

—IRVIN S. COBB, U.S. JOURNALIST AND HUMORIST

# EULOGIZE (BUT DON'T PLAGIARIZE)

If your chosen eulogist needs inspiration to craft their speech, there's plenty of material out there to draw from. (We're talking structure and themes here, not straight-up plagiarism. Your mourners will probably give the claims in your eulogy the benefit of the doubt, but they definitely won't believe you were the first person to scale Mount Everest.) Following are excerpts from some of the best eulogies of all time. Why can't yours be one of them?

**ROSA PARKS**'s eulogy by Oprah Winfrey was a powerful tribute from one incredible Black woman who helped change the world to another.

*After our first meeting I realized that God uses good people to do great things. And I'm here today to say a final thank-you, Sister Rosa, for being a great woman who used your life to serve, to serve us all. That day that you refused to give up your seat on the bus, you, Sister Rosa, changed the trajectory of my life and the lives of so many other people in the world. I would not be standing here today nor standing where I stand every day had she not chosen to sit down.*

**GRAHAM CHAPMAN**'s eulogy by John Cleese is exactly as side-splitting as you would expect for a eulogy from one Monty Python member to another.

*Graham Chapman, co-author of the "Parrot Sketch," is no more. He has ceased to be, bereft of life, he rests in peace, he has kicked the bucket, hopped the twig, bit the dust, snuffed it, breathed his last, and gone to meet the Great Head of Light Entertainment in the sky, and I guess that we're all thinking how sad it is that a man of such talent, such capability and kindness, of such intelligence should now be so suddenly spirited away at the age of only forty-eight, before he'd achieved many of the things of which he was capable, and before he'd had enough fun.*

*Well, I feel that I should say, "Nonsense. Good riddance to him, the freeloading bastard! I hope he fries."*

**CRAIG SAGER** was a famous sports reporter. When he died in 2016, his daughter wasn't afraid to tell it like it is in her hilarious (yet touching) eulogy.

*Over the past couple years, and especially in the last few days, I've been overwhelmed by all the lovely things that everyone has had to say about my father. And I just keep thinking to myself, "Have any of these people ever even met him?"*

*I heard that he lived his life with grace. Grace? Really? We are talking about a man who hopped a fence while streaking at the Kentucky Derby and tore open his . . . whatever the church-appropriate euphemism for balls is. Hardly graceful.*

**STEVE JOBS**'s eulogy by his sister Mona Simpson reminds us that no matter how much we accomplish, there's always unfinished business we'll leave behind.

*None of us knows for certain how long we'll be here. On Steve's better days, even in the last year, he embarked upon projects and elicited promises from his friends at Apple to finish them. Some boat builders in the Netherlands have a gorgeous stainless-steel hull ready to be covered with the finishing wood. His three daughters remain unmarried, his two youngest still girls, and he'd wanted to walk them down the aisle as he'd walked me the day of my wedding.*

*We all—in the end—die in medias res. In the middle of a story. Of many stories.*

*I suppose it's not quite accurate to call the death of someone who lived with cancer for years unexpected, but Steve's death was unexpected for us.*

*What I learned from my brother's death was that character is essential: what he was, was how he died.*

"If you carefully consider what you want to be said of you in the funeral experience, you will find your definition of success."

—STEPHEN COVEY, AUTHOR OF
*THE 7 HABITS OF HIGHLY EFFECTIVE PEOPLE*

# My EULOGY

The best parts of every eulogy are the stories about the deceased. In a lot of ways, a eulogy is like a best man's speech, but hopefully with fewer sex jokes.

Don't count on hope, though. What are the anecdotes from your life that you'd like to be included in your eulogy? They can be big triumphs or small, personal moments. Think of what really captures the essence of you. What are the key things you want people to know about you after you're gone? Use the space below to describe the top three anecdotes, messages, or accomplishments you'd like to be relayed in your eulogy.

1.

2.

3.

# Funeral Readings

Not everyone is able to take the pain, relief, and existential dread that they feel at the death of a loved one and weave those emotions into words that express exactly what they want to say about the deceased. Unless your family is full of English professors, they might not be able to quickly jot down an emotional testament to your death that captures the moment and touches everyone at your funeral.

Thankfully, some very talented people have done that work already and it's perfectly acceptable to have someone read their brilliant and tear-jerking efforts instead. Consider the following poignant extracts from poems, speeches, and plays for your ultimate bedtime story.

From *The Tempest* by William Shakespeare:

> *Our revels are now ended. These our actors,*
> *As I foretold you, were all spirits and*
> *Are melted into air, into thin air:*
> *And, like the baseless fabric of this vision,*
> *The cloud-capp'd towers, the gorgeous palaces,*
> *The solemn temples, the great globe itself,*
> *Yea, all which it inherit, shall dissolve*
> *And, like this insubstantial pageant faded,*
> *Leave not a rack behind. We are such stuff*
> *As dreams are made on, and our little life*
> *Is rounded in a sleep.*

From "The King of Terrors" by Henry Scott Holland:

> *Death is nothing at all. It does not count. I have only slipped away into the next room. Nothing has happened. Everything remains exactly as it was. I am I, and you are you, and the old life that we lived so fondly together is untouched, unchanged. Whatever we were*

to each other, that we are still. Call me by the old familiar name. Speak of me in the easy way which you always used. Put no difference into your tone. Wear no forced air of solemnity or sorrow. Laugh as we always laughed at the little jokes that we enjoyed together. Play, smile, think of me, pray for me. Let my name be ever the household word that it always was. Let it be spoken without an effort, without the ghost of a shadow upon it.

"When I am dead, my dearest" by Christina Rossetti:

When I am dead, my dearest,
Sing no sad songs for me;
Plant thou no roses at my head,
Nor shady cypress tree:
Be the green grass above me
With showers and dewdrops wet;
And if thou wilt, remember,
And if thou wilt, forget.
I shall not see the shadows,
I shall not feel the rain;
I shall not hear the nightingale
Sing on, as if in pain:
And dreaming through the twilight
That doth not rise nor set,
Haply I may remember,
And haply may forget.

If none of those passages seem to hit the nail perfectly on the head, you should also have a look at:

"DEATH" by Joe Brainard

"DO NOT GO GENTLE INTO THAT GOOD NIGHT" by Dylan Thomas

"DO NOT STAND AT MY GRAVE AND WEEP" by Mary Elizabeth Frye

"FUNERAL BLUES" by W. H. Auden

"DEATH BE NOT PROUD" by John Donne

"HOW DO I LOVE THEE?" by Elizabeth Barrett Browning

"[I CARRY YOUR HEART WITH ME(I CARRY IT IN]" by e. e. cummings

"ODE: INTIMATIONS OF IMMORTALITY FROM RECOLLECTIONS OF EARLY CHILDHOOD" by William Wordsworth

"SHE IS GONE" by David Harkins

"TO REMEMBER ME" by Robert N. Test

Of course, if you're religious, excerpts from your faith's holy text(s) are worth considering (for Christians, for example, Psalm 23 is a standard). Many people choose novel excerpts as well; many classic books—including *Fahrenheit 451*, *Charlotte's Web*, *No Matter What* by Debi Gliori, *The Velveteen Rabbit*, *The Little Prince*, the Harry Potter series, and the Lord of the Rings series—have something to say about death. Be sure to consider anything that's meaningful to you, whether that's a poem you composed yourself, a favorite quote from a film or play, or song lyrics.

# My FUNERAL READINGS

List or transcribe the poems or passages that you'd like to be read at your funeral below. Consider the kind of tone you'd like to strike. Can you have some readings that are deep and meaningful and another that will make your mourners laugh through their tears? They don't all have to be about death, either. Maybe there's a passage that has meaning to you for another reason, for example, because it was read at your wedding or comes from your favorite book.

Also consider who you would like to deliver each reading. For many people, reading a prepared piece might be easier and less stressful than composing and delivering a eulogy. You can record your selections here or on the "My Funeral Dream Team" worksheet, page 84.

# Funeral Music

Just like your high school prom, the theme of your funeral is encompassed in the songs played. This is, after all, your last dance. Death has been trying to catch your eye this whole time, and now you are going to sway together with no gym teacher to yell at you for getting too close.

Let's stop torturing that metaphor and just say: the music at your funeral is your swan song. The first notes might be the moment when even the most stiff-lipped mourner bursts into tears. Music and funerals are both full of emotion, and as such they complement each other perfectly.

## CLASSIC SONGS

Here are some classic funeral songs to consider:

"AMAZING GRACE" by John Newton

"CANDLE IN THE WIND" by Elton John

"CANDLE ON THE WATER" by Al Kasha and Joel Hirschhorn

"DANNY BOY" by Frederic E. Weatherly

"HALLELUJAH" by Leonard Cohen
(or the Jeff Buckley cover, if you are of a certain age)

"I WILL ALWAYS LOVE YOU" by Dolly Parton
(the Whitney Houston version works better if you plan on a pyrotechnic display during the last, impressively belted chorus)

"OVER THE RAINBOW" by Harold Arlen

"WHEN THE SAINTS GO MARCHING IN" by Louis Armstrong

"YOU'LL NEVER WALK ALONE" by Rodgers and Hammerstein
(the cover by Gerry and the Pacemakers is particularly good for Liverpool F.C. supporters)

## CHEEKY SONGS

Now let's look beyond the classics. Toward the beginning of the 2003 romantic comedy *Love Actually*, Liam Neeson's character says farewell to his dead wife at her funeral. At her request, he sends her off to the Bay City Rollers cover of "Bye, Bye, Baby (Baby Goodbye)" originally by The Four Seasons.

Other slightly tongue-in-cheek but appropriate song options include:

"ALWAYS LOOK ON THE BRIGHT SIDE OF LIFE" by Eric Idle

"(DON'T FEAR) THE REAPER" by Blue Öyster Cult
(consider requesting that the cowbell portion of the song be played live)

"DON'T YOU (FORGET ABOUT ME)" by Simple Minds

"SPIRIT IN THE SKY" by Norman Greenbaum

## LIVE MUSIC

Finally, there is always the live music option. If you hire someone to sing "Ave Maria," make sure they are actually talented. You don't want all the mourners at your funeral to be stifling laughter as your daughter-in-law who never made it on Broadway strains to hit the high notes.

Harpists are also popular, and nothing could be classier. If you want to make a statement at your funeral—that statement being "Look how super fancy I am even now that I am dead"—and force the philistines in your family to sit through some culture they have no way of politely escaping from, a live harpist is perfect.

Bagpipes are another classic choice, especially if you are Scottish or have Scottish heritage (or at least pretend you do). The problem is: bagpipes divide the crowd. On the one hand, they have a strong connection to funerals, and the image of a kilted man standing ramrod straight and playing a dirge on the bagpipes is iconic. On the other hand, many people freaking hate the sound of bagpipes. However, if your bagpipe-hating nemesis will be in attendance, this could be your chance for one final dig.

# A CELEBRITY PERFORMER TO ENTERTAIN YOUR MOURNERS

**H**aving family or friends sing a moving hymn at your funeral is great, but we all know you'd throw them out on their derrières if you could get a celebrity performer instead. There's no aiming too high! Here's some inspiration:

- Christina Aguilera sang "At Last" at Etta James's funeral in 2012.

- Alicia Keys sang "Send Me an Angel" at Whitney Houston's funeral in 2012.

- Who didn't perform at Michael Jackson's 2009 funeral? It basically doubled as one of the greatest concerts of all time, with performances by Stevie Wonder, Lionel Richie, Mariah Carey, Jennifer Hudson, Usher, and more.

- Aretha Franklin's 2018 funeral drew more performers than the corpse had costume changes. (Did you know that's an option for your own funeral? The Queen of Soul made it so.) These included Faith Hill, Ariana Grande, Smokey Robinson, Jennifer Hudson, Chaka Khan, Gladys Knight, and Stevie Wonder, among many others.

Of course, all these famous artists were performing at the (televised) funerals of other celebrities. If you haven't managed to become a celebrity by the time you die, first of all, what were you wasting all that time on? But there's still a chance that a famous performer will agree to play your funeral. One option is to write a moving letter, to be delivered to your favorite artist after you pass on, in the hopes it will convince them to sing at the funeral of a random stranger.[*]

---

[*] If that doesn't work, consider offering them money. Plenty of artists have performed for murderous dictators as long as the price was right.

# My FINAL PLAYLIST

List the top five songs you'd like to be played at your funeral service. In the notes section, include the reasons why you chose it. Did you dance to it at your wedding? See the band live at the best concert of your life? Awkwardly lose your virginity as it played on the car radio? Even if the song holds no special significance, perhaps the lyrics stand out for you. Also consider which version you prefer, if there are multiple, and whether you'd like the song to be performed live or recorded. (If you have a live performer in mind, you can record them here or on the "My Funeral Dream Team" worksheet, page 84.)

**SONG TITLE**_____
**NOTES**_____
_____

**SONG TITLE**_____
**NOTES**_____
_____

**SONG TITLE**_____
**NOTES**_____
_____

**SONG TITLE**_____
**NOTES**_____
_____

**SONG TITLE**_____
**NOTES**_____
_____

**SONG TITLE**_____
**NOTES**_____
_____

# My "DO NOT PLAY" LIST

Since music is so personal, there are plenty of songs you might want to include on a "Definitely Don't Play this Crap at My Funeral" list for your loved ones to reference. For example, John Lennon's "Imagine" might seem like a great choice to your next of kin, but not if you're secretly one of the many people who think it's hypocritical slop.

Fill out your "Do Not Play" list below. If you need some examples, consider these songs to avoid (unless you have a very particular type of humor):

"**DING-DONG! THE WITCH IS DEAD**" by HAROLD ARLEN
"**STAYIN' ALIVE**" by THE BEE GEES
"**CELEBRATION**" by KOOL & THE GANG
"**ANOTHER ONE BITES THE DUST**" by QUEEN
"**HIGHWAY TO HELL**" by AC/DC

SONG TITLE_____

SONG TITLE_____

SONG TITLE_____

SONG TITLE_____

SONG TITLE_____

SONG TITLE_____

SONG TITLE_____

SONG TITLE_____

SONG TITLE_____

SONG TITLE_____

# RENT-A-MOURNER

If you're worried no one will show up to your funeral, ask yourself, what would Jesus do? Well, according to the Bible, he might hire professional mourners. Paying people to come to your funeral and cry gets mentioned in the Good Book a *lot*. (Your Sunday school teacher probably didn't mention it, though.) Historically, cultures in China, Egypt, India, and the Middle East thought that hiring mourners for a funeral was a great idea. Ideally, they'd be women, who were considered better performers than men—more willing and able to "go there" emotionally.

The idea was that mourners wailing and following the coffin in big groups made the deceased look more important and more loved, and also that hearing and seeing other people cry—even professional fakers—would help real mourners achieve their own emotional release. It's not a terrible idea when you frame it that way. The practice continues to this day in parts of China and Egypt. Until 2019, there was even a U.K. company called Rent A Mourner, which had to shut down when it became too popular and couldn't handle all the business.

If you find that hiring professional mourners is too expensive or unavailable in your area, consider the offer made by author Dana Schwartz on Twitter in 2019: "If you pay me $50 I'll show up to your funeral but stand really far away, holding a black umbrella regardless of the weather, so that people think you died with a dark and interesting secret."

# JAZZ FUNERALS

New Orleans jazzman Sidney Bechet once said, "Music here is as much a part of death as it is of life." The city has a novel way of sending off musicians, notable residents, or, lately, anyone who wants one, no matter where they live: the jazz funeral. Notables like David Bowie, Fats Domino, and Jim Henson all got the jazz funeral treatment.

The tradition comes from Black culture in New Orleans, where African spiritual practices mixed with the military and colonial traditions of the city. For a few decades in the early twentieth century, many white people turned their noses up at jazz funerals, but Black citizens continued their funeral celebrations, and by the 1960s, people of all races and religions were participating in the tradition.

Jazz funerals have two very different parts. When leaving the home or church for the cemetery, a brass band leads the coffin, often in a glass-sided hearse pulled by a white mule, playing mournful hymns or spirituals along the way. But once the deceased has been buried or interred, the tone immediately changes. Not because everyone is happy they can forget about death until the next funeral, but because the deceased is believed to have gone to glory in heaven. The band leads the now-jubilant mourners back through the streets, playing up-tempo tunes like "When the Saints Go Marching In" and dancing, often with parasols and handkerchiefs. Even strangers who encounter a jazz funeral are welcome to join in.

# PHOTO FINISH

The Victorians often waited until after a loved one died to go to the trouble and expense of getting a picture of them. These postmortem photos are eerie, and obviously the subject doesn't always look their best.

These days we have the opposite problem. We have so many photos of ourselves, on so many devices, posted on social media and even, very occasionally, displayed in photo albums. And you and your grieving loved ones might have very different ideas of which ones are most flattering.

Print out your favorite photos and include them here, or leave a digital roadmap of where to find them. (A folder on your computer labeled "Photos Where I Look Super Hot to Use After I'm Dead" would be perfect.) Remember, these photos will get lots of use. There's the obituary, the social media posts, a poster at your funeral, and more. If you die in a way that's exciting/tragic/bizarre enough to make the news, these images will be splashed across screens and front pages around the world. So only choose the ones where you look your absolute best.

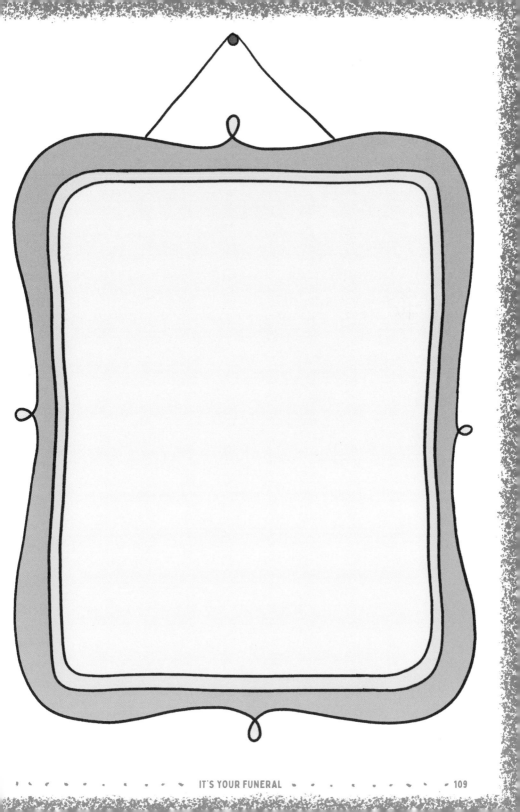

# Setting a Selfie Policy

Look, your friends and family may love you a lot, but they love their phones even more. You can ask them to leave their smartphones in the car, or turn them off, or for the love of God at least put them on silent, but you are fighting a losing battle. There is a good chance your eulogy will be interrupted by various text and email notifications. (And let's be honest, you understand. There's a good chance there's a cell phone in your coffin or urn. See "Cell Phones," page 58.)

While people have been taking pictures of and with dead bodies since the very beginning of photography, the existence of camera phones means taking selfies at a funeral is a brave new world of etiquette. There are plenty of people who will proudly pose with your corpse, given the chance. No matter how fashionable your outfit or how good a job the makeup artist did, you might not be thrilled if you show up on social media looking a bit gray. You can assume your loved ones would never do such a thing, but if you want to be sure, consider hanging a flashing neon NO PHOTOS sign over your coffin.

On the other extreme, if you want to encourage photography and unleash the full creativity of your guests, I've got two words for you: green screen.

# REWARDING YOUR FUNERAL GUESTS

**S**ure, you can pay people to come to your funeral, cutting them a check beforehand to make sure they mourn extra good (see "Rent-a-Mourner," page 106). But what if instead of hiring pros, you just want to reward the amateur mourners who attend with no other incentive than their love for you? (Or, in the case of your nemesis, to make sure you are actually dead?) Wisconsin business owner Dennis Valstad decided to add a line to his will declaring that $500,000 would be split evenly between everyone who attended his funeral. Then he didn't tell a soul.

He must have been a great guy in other ways, because 267 people showed up to send him off when he died in 2019. A couple months later, they all received letters saying they were in the money. Each attendee got a check for $1,872, from the pastor to the organist to the children attendees.

You don't need half a million bucks lying around to reward or thank your guests. Maybe note in your will that everyone gets enough cash for a pizza on you. And then hope it gives your nemesis food poisoning.

# My GUEST LIST and PEST LIST

Most people leave the funeral guest list to their loved ones, trusting them to know all the important individuals to invite, but . . . well, we all have secrets. Maybe there are people out there whom you want to have at your funeral, but unless you leave instructions, no one will think to invite them. Perhaps it's a long-lost sibling. A cousin you disowned once he got involved in Amway. A secret second family you maintained through years of lies about being a traveling salesman (shame on you!). List their names and contact information here, so they too can say their goodbyes when the time comes.

**NAME**_____

**ADDRESS**_____

**PHONE**_____

**EMAIL**_____


**NAME**_____

**ADDRESS**_____

**PHONE**_____

**EMAIL**_____


**NAME**_____

**ADDRESS**_____

**PHONE**_____

**EMAIL**_____


**NAME**_____

**ADDRESS**_____

**PHONE**_____

**EMAIL**_____


**NAME**_____

**ADDRESS**_____

**PHONE**_____

**EMAIL**_____

Of course, there is also the opposite problem. You may not want to give your nemesis the pleasure of seeing you laid in the ground. In that case, add some names to this DO NOT INVITE list. Include anyone you have secretly hated all these years, anyone who owes you money, and maybe a few random names just to leave some drama in your wake.

Add the name and reason for being uninvited to each mugshot. You may also paste in a photo of the offender's face if desired.

# Lightening the Mood

While the stereotypical funeral is black, dour, and sad, there's no law that it has to be that way. Maybe you're a funny person and you want that reflected in your send-off. That's what Irishman Shay Bradley did in 2019. As his family and friends stood at his graveside, they heard a voice . . . coming from inside the coffin.

Bradley seemed to be calling out, "Hello, hello—let me out! Where the fuck am I? Let me out, let me out! It's fucking dark in here. Is that the priest I can hear? This is Shay, I'm in the box. No, in fucking front of you. I'm dead." Then he started singing.

Thankfully, he wasn't being buried alive; he was really and truly dead. (Wait, which of those is worse?) Even more thankfully, no one had a heart attack when they heard Bradley yelling. With the help of his children, Bradley had pranked them all. Everyone left the funeral laughing, and footage of the incident went viral online.

Humans love to laugh about death (otherwise this book wouldn't exist), so don't be afraid to arrange a funny funeral. For example, if you think fart jokes are the epitome of humor, leave instructions to have whoopee cushions placed on all the seats. Your loved ones will probably expect nothing less.

# How to LIGHTEN THE MOOD

Include a few ideas below, as well as instructions for your loved ones to help them carry it off.

# Planning Your Eternal Rest

As much as you might want to plan a never-ending end-of-life service so everyone has a chance to say all the great things they will definitely want to say about you, at some point that portion of the funeral ends. Then it's time for the main event—the thing our very distant ancestors invented funerals for in the first place: getting rid of the body (or cremains or what-have-you). The basics haven't changed much, but even if you want to follow tradition, there are plenty of ways to put your personal stamp on this part of your funeral, whether your remains are heading six feet under, under the sea, or to the freaking moon.

## INTERMENT: In You Go

Let's assume you've chosen to be buried, either in a coffin or via natural burial, or to be cremated and have your remains interred rather than scattered. In that case there are some common rituals and logistics that accompany putting your body in the ground.

If you plan to have your burial immediately following the funeral service, there will usually be a procession to the cemetery. A hearse will transport your body, typically with your closest family and friends following in cars behind. If you've been cremated, you won't need your own special transportation, and your urn can be carried by a relative.

However, many people have the burial at a later time, not immediately following the service. This may be down to scheduling conflicts, like when the burial plot will be ready versus when all your loved ones can make it to a service.* These are the sort of logistics you have think about, even if your death is going to be so far in the future it's impossible to know what day everyone can get off work.

If you are a member of the military or a veteran, consider any ceremonial aspects you want performed at the graveside. This can include folding the flag that draped the coffin and giving it to your family, a bugler sounding "Taps," and a twenty-

---

* In some areas, delays might even be due to the weather. In extremely cold climates, like Siberia or northern Canada, the ground can literally be frozen solid, meaning bodies need to be stored until warmer weather brings a thaw.

one-gun salute. If you plan on being buried in a private cemetery rather than a national cemetery, you may have to ask the local Veterans Administration or the funeral home to make sure these honors are performed.

Once the coffin is at the graveside, traditionally it remains closed the whole time. A notable exception is Eastern Orthodox funerals. In that tradition, the coffin lid is opened one final time right before burial, so people can say their ultimate goodbye. But anyone of any religion (or no religion) can also incorporate this into their funeral.

The coffin is then lowered into the grave. (This can be delayed until everyone has left, if you prefer, but it often happens while guests are present.) The family may throw flowers or clumps of dirt onto the coffin in a final act of mourning. The assembled guests usually leave before the coffin is actually buried under the remaining dirt.

There is also the option of forgoing a funeral service in a house of worship or other venue and holding the entire affair graveside. This makes the logistics a bit simpler and often means a shorter service overall. You can still retain the eulogy and other aspects of a larger service, but in a more intimate setting.

# SCATTERING: *Away You Go*

Scatterings have fewer formal traditions associated with them in the West, simply because they haven't been happening for as long. However, people in places like the U.S. and Europe are embracing all different types of ceremonies, including:

- **FLOATING CEREMONIES:** *a biodegradable urn is floated out on a body of water*

- **SKY CEREMONIES:** *a plane or drone scatters the ashes*

- **RINGING CEREMONIES:** *the ashes are spread in a circle around a tree*

In India, Hindus traditionally cremate their dead by the Ganges River and then immerse the ashes in the sacred waters. In Japan, cremation usually happens after the funeral. The family then picks the bones out of the ashes with chopsticks, starting with the feet and moving up. The cremains can be divided between more than one urn, and urns are traditionally buried in a family grave, temple, or com-

pany grave (although in the modern day, anything goes). So while you may want to create your own original ceremony for when your ashes are scattered, there are plenty of existing traditions to draw from.

However, keep in mind the logistical issues that can arise when scattering ashes. As the International Ash Scattering Society (yes, that's a real thing) so succinctly put it in a blog post, "STAND UPWIND"—or else you risk a *Big Lebowski*–esque debacle. They also note a man who died while trying to scatter ashes and fly a plane at the same time, and warn that people who insist on scattering ashes at Disneyland can be arrested if caught. If you ask your loved ones to travel somewhere far away to scatter the ashes, tell them to keep the luggage containing your cremains with them at all times, or you might get lost by the airline. Can you imagine a less dignified end?

It's also perfectly acceptable to skip a scattering ceremony altogether—perhaps you want your ashes to rest on your spouse's or child's mantle or in a shrine in the living room you shared with a loved one. (And you wouldn't be alone—according to survey in California and Washington State, one in five people are storing ashes in their homes!)

## EVERYTHING ELSE: *Wherever You Go*

If you have chosen a less traditional manner of disposing of your body: What kind of ceremony to dispose of your remains will be possible? For example, if you have decided to become part of a coral reef, would you like family members to be there when you are placed on the ocean floor? How many people do you know who can scuba dive?

If there won't be any remains of you to inter or scatter (for example, if you're being plastinated; see page 45), it's perfectly fine to skip this portion of the funeral service altogether. Alternately, you could ask your family to inter an empty coffin or scatter ashes that are symbolic of you if the ritual brings them comfort. (Bonus: there's even more room for grave goods in an empty coffin!)

# My ETERNAL REST

Use the space below to describe your vision of your final interment, scattering, or what-have-you. Be sure to consider not only meaningful gestures or rituals (i.e., a twenty-one-gun salute, or the type of flowers you'd like placed on your coffin) but logistical concerns as well. Will your family need to rent a plane or apply for permits? Would you prefer close family only to attend, or a public ceremony?

Perhaps most important, where would you like to be laid to rest? If you're being buried, you might have a family plot or local cemetery in mind. If you're being scattered, the possibilities are practically infinite. Think of the most meaningful places in your life. Would it be possible to scatter your ashes at any of these locations? If so, include a note about why the place you've selected means so much to you.

# PART THREE

# IT'S YOUR

# *Legacy*

# DON'T YOU FORGET ABOUT ME
## (EVER)

Yes, funerals are the landmark event that define saying goodbye to a person and accepting that they are gone. But obviously we don't forget about someone once the funeral's over—or at least not right away. Most people's existence fades into the mists of time eventually. It's almost more terrifying than dying: the thought that, one day, your whole life will likely be forgotten.

Take a moment to gaze existentially out the window . . .

Back now? Great. In this section, we're going to make sure that such an existentially terrifying thing never happens. As Terry Pratchett wrote, "Do you not know that a man is not dead while his name is still spoken?" Sure, you could guarantee that people will always talk about you by becoming president, but that's a lot of work.

Fortunately, there are plenty of less taxing ways to make sure you're remembered long past your expiration date. From your obituary and grave marker to your material legacy and those more ethereal parts of your heritage, it's important to make sure your effect on the world lasts long after your perfect funeral is over.

# Marking Your Postmortem Territory

The easiest way to make sure people keep speaking your name is to have an awesome memorial to yourself. Whether it's a tombstone, a plaque, a memorial bench, or a giant rock, you can leave behind a monument to your existence that is so great, people will see it generations from now and say, "Wow, this person must have been really cool." And just in case a slab of rock alone isn't evocative enough to help people sum up your complex essence, that's where your epitaph comes in. Mourners, fans, and pilgrims will come for the memorial and stay because the tagline of your life touched them on a deeper level.

Boom, immortality. Just like that. So you see how important this is. Let's learn how you can be remembered and ensure that you live on forever.

## HEADSTONES: *You-Are-Dead Stones*

Headstones (or tombstones or gravestones—they're all the same thing) go back to at least 3000 BCE. Back then, they really were stones, massive ones, that did little more than mark the location of a grave with numerous bodies in it. By the 1650s CE, Europeans started burying their dead in churchyards on a regular basis and using more modern-looking headstones to mark the graves. Then the Victorians came along and put their own stamp on headstones, as they did with every other facet of death and dying. The Victorian era is when it became common for people in the U.S. and most of Western Europe, no matter how poor, to memorialize their dead—usually with a gravestone that was inscribed with the name and dates of the deceased, as well as a nice epitaph that said a bit about them.

We all know the standard shape for a headstone: a half circle on top of a rectangle. But headstones come in all shapes, sizes, and materials. Some are crosses or other religious symbols. Simple, flat grave markers are also popular, and this understated variety is mandated by some religions or sects, like Quakers and Islam. But sometimes a person will have a larger memorial built that still counts as a headstone, if one that's so thirsty for attention you're embarrassed for it. The tallest headstone in America is thought to be a 150-foot obelisk over the grave of

Thomas Evans, a Philadelphia dentist who died in 1897. The smallest headstone, if you want to go the other way for either humble or financial reasons, is thought to be that of Linnie Crouch of Missouri, who died one year after the dentist. Her grave marker is just six inches by five inches and can be flipped over to read both sides, since there wasn't room for all the information on just one.

## CRYPTS: *Not as Creepy as They Sound*

Crypts weren't always places to stash dead bodies. To the ancient Romans, a crypt was any vaulted room at least partially underground, which could mean a storage cellar, a horse stall, or even a sewer. But Christians used those various types of crypts to store their dead back around the third century CE, when their religion was illegal, and the tradition continued from there. By medieval times, crypts were purpose-built stone rooms beneath the floors of churches, where the sarcophagi of important people and the relics of saints were stored.

Although the crypts of all those fancy medieval churches filled up long ago, you still have the option to be laid to rest in a modern crypt. Some cemeteries may have one where many unrelated bodies are laid to rest. This can be a money-saving idea, since it's often cheaper for the cemetery to simply open a crypt than dig a new grave. But if you want a dedicated crypt for your family (like many royal clans have), or even just for you so your ghost and/or zombie has lots of room to stretch out, that will cost some serious coin.

Underground crypts have a romantic element to them, though. There's something darkly gothic about descending into a crypt, never to return. And having your family all together one day, in dry conditions, is a lovely thought.

## MAUSOLEUMS: *Fit for a King*

Named for a Persian ruler who built himself a super-fancy building to be dead in (see "Iconic Funerary Monuments," page 130), mausoleums have real gravitas. Which means they also have a massive price tag.

Mausoleums are large structures that house the coffin that contains the body, like mortality Matryoshka dolls. This means you can have statues, your name, friezes, anything you can dream of carved in stone on the outside of your personal death shed. And instead of being buried, you'll be "entombed" within the building.

In some places that are prone to flooding, such as New Orleans, mausoleums are more common than graves. But in most other areas, unless you're willing to spend a lot to have yourself entombed, you might want to look into a public mausoleum that has room for you, or garden mausoleums, in which a crypt for each casket is located on the outside of the building (that kind of mausoleum isn't walk-in). The six-figure way is to have one built special for you (and your family, if they ask nicely). Sometimes they're erected on private land, since if you have hundreds of thousands of dollars to invest in a private mausoleum, you probably have an estate with acres of rolling hills, too. Otherwise, some cemeteries will allow you to build on their property.

If you plan to be cremated but like the sound of a mausoleum, there's a version for urns called a columbarium. Almost always of the public variety, rather than built for just one person's or one family's cremains, these buildings have niches (on the inside or on the outside) where urns are placed and marked with a plaque.

Most of the famous funerary monuments around the world can be classified as mausoleums (see page 130). So if you want to be remembered forever, this method has a lot of potential—but start saving now.

# FUNERARY SCULPTURE: *Death of the Artist*

Funerary art, particularly sculpture, is often so beautiful that later generations remove it from the grave and display it in private homes or museums. Should you choose to be remembered this way, that is a danger you'll have to either accept or plan for (think: booby traps).

An early form of funerary sculpture was the tomb effigy. If you've ever seen the final resting place of a medieval king or queen, you know the type, where the deceased is sculpted on their sarcophagus lid out of metal, wood, or stone. When it comes to freestanding statues, there have been various fads throughout history, including the nineteenth-century American mania for carved stone chairs (it probably made sense at the time). Stone urns, pillars, weeping women, and angels (weeping or otherwise) are common sights in graveyards. But you can be laid to rest under a sculpted guitar, computer, book, car—literally anything that can be represented through art.*

The award for most interesting use of funerary sculpture in the modern era has to go to John Milburn Davis of Kansas. When his wife Sarah died, she was buried under a regular headstone. But a few years later, in 1932, John decided to kick things up a notch. He spent four years and his life savings having eleven life-size statues carved of himself and Sarah (along with some chairs, because if the Victorians did it, it must be a good idea), all sheltered by a marble canopy. The statues show the couple aging, and then John alone, missing both an arm and Sarah (the missing arm was due to a farm accident that had nothing to do with her death). John was proud of his mini sculpture garden and would hang around the cemetery explaining it to visitors until he died in 1947. The townsfolk hated it at the time, but now the display has become a popular tourist attraction. So if you select a sculpture to adorn your grave and your family says it's a bit extravagant, tell them to get their butts to Kansas before they gripe to you about it.

---

* Except a penis. The cemetery probably won't be okay with a penis statue (but you never know!).

## MEMORIAL BENCHES: *All the Good Seats Are Taken*

When it comes to a memorial that reminds tired people you once lived and they owe their ability to rest for a moment to the fact that you don't anymore, there's nothing better than a memorial bench. If your loved ones will be putting your bench on private land, or over your grave in a cemetery, then your options are limited only by your imagination. Your memorial bench can be made of wood, stone, or metal. It can display a plaque with information about you or have your name, dates, and epitaph carved into the bench itself. It can be simple or elaborate, meant to be comfortable or meant to make a statement.

But if you want a memorial bench in a public place, there is more red tape. Usually, you will be limited to a small plaque on a predetermined bench. You probably won't be allowed to display your famous catchphrase, "Fuck off, you fuckers." The best locations for public benches might already be taken by people who beat you by dying first. And the most exclusive locations can be pricey. Adopting a bench in Central Park, for example, costs $10,000. But if it means a lost tourist thinks of you for a moment while they sit on your bench and cry, knowing their mother was right and they aren't cut out for the big city, it will truly be worth it.

## MEMORIAL PLAQUES: *Memories Everywhere*

A memorial plaque can be placed almost anywhere, from a theater seat, to your spot at the bar, to your alma mater, to the tree over your grave (see "Tree Burial," page 31), to the place where your ashes are scattered or interred. Anywhere your loved ones can get permission, basically. And since the financial outlay is usually minimal, you can even put a plaque in all those places, thus ensuring the maximum number of people will read your name for years to come. Plaques are also infinitely customizable and can include personal details about you, an engraving of your face, your favorite quote—whatever your heart desires! Plaques can be made of any material, but bronze, brass, and stainless steel are popular choices.

In some cases, a "plaque" might actually be a brick. For example, if you're a Green Bay Packers fan, you can be memorialized on a brick at Lambeau Field for as little as $50. (If you hate the Cheeseheads and all that they stand for, most other sports teams have similar deals.)

# ICONIC FUNERARY MONUMENTS

Even the biggest, most elaborate, most eye-catching grave marker on the market today will have nothing on some of the most famous funeral monuments of all time. In fact, one was so impressive that it gave its name to all the others. The Mausoleum at Halicarnassus (in modern-day Turkey) was named after the dead ruler it was built for. Mausolus began planning his monument before his death, around 350 BCE, and his wife made sure building continued after he died. When she died before it was finished, the workers kept on going because they knew they were making something incredible. The result stood 138 feet high and was covered in columns, dozens of statues, and intricate bas-reliefs depicting scenes from Greek mythology. It made the list of the Seven Wonders of the Ancient World, only to be destroyed by earthquakes in the 1400s.

Fortunately, another even older example of the Seven Wonders is still around. The Great Pyramid of Khufu, the oldest and largest of the pyramids of Giza, was built as a tomb for the aforementioned pharaoh 4,500 years ago. When you want to be remembered forever, plopping a 481-foot-tall pyramid in the middle of a desert is one way to do it.

Planning your own giant memorial is the best way to ensure you get what you want, but not everyone is so inclined. Fortunately, some have family members who will do it for them. When Mumtaz Mahal died, her husband, the Mughal emperor Shah Jahan, was so crushed that he built the Taj Mahal to house her tomb.

Still, unless you trust your relatives to spend dozens of years and boatloads of money to construct one of the most defining architectural pieces of all time, better count on doing it yourself.

# Epitaphs

Few things are as important as your epitaph. It tells the person standing at your grave, niche, or memorial: "This is who I was and when I was here. That's all that matters." And it may be the only thing about your life that's remembered hundreds of years from now. There's often so little space available that many people just go with the classic name and date combination, or sort of spice it up with phrases like "Here Lies" or "Rest in Peace." A simple description of a person's main role or achievement in life might be included, like "Loving Mother" or "Winner of the 2032 Bad Sex in Fiction Award." Short Bible verses, quotes, and song lyrics are popular as well.

But consider adding something a bit more. This is your final statement to the world. Let the message on your tombstone or memorial plaque tell mourners for generations to come who you were. If you need inspiration, there are plenty of notable epitaphs from those who went before you.

## MOVING EPITAPHS

Some people (or their loved ones or admirers) chose moving epitaphs that sum up the deceased's essence in only a few words.

> "Free at last, free at last, thank God almighty I'm free at last."
>
> —MARTIN LUTHER KING JR.

The Reverend King ended his famous "I Have a Dream" speech with lyrics from a Black spiritual hymn, and the quote fittingly became his epitaph.

> "When I was in the military they gave me a medal for killing two men and a discharge for loving one."
>
> —LEONARD MATLOVICH

This Purple Heart–decorated airman was the first gay member of the U.S. military to publicly out himself, and he fought for the rights of gay service members until his death from complications of HIV/AIDS in 1988.

"The best is yet to come."

—FRANK SINATRA

Sinatra's epitaph is taken from the title of a popular song he recorded on his 1964 album *It Might as Well Be Swing*. It was the last song he ever performed in public.

## POETIC EPITAPHS

Some people (often writers) leave behind lyrical or philosophical statements, for the mourner at the grave to consider while they reflect on life and death.

"Death is the enemy. Against you I will fling myself, unvanquished and unyielding o Death! The waves broke on the shore."

—VIRGINIA WOOLF

The words on Woolf's memorial plaque are from her novel *The Waves*, but they took on new meaning when she died by suicide in the River Ouse.

"Called back."

—EMILY DICKINSON

These were the last words Dickinson wrote in a letter before she died, as well as the title of one of her favorite books.

"I had a lover's quarrel with the world"

—ROBERT FROST

More than two decades before he died, Frost wrote the poem "A Lesson for Today," which ended with a short verse explaining this should be written on his tombstone.

> "So we beat on, boats against the current,
> borne back ceaselessly into the past."
>
> —F. SCOTT FITZGERALD AND ZELDA FITZGERALD

The author of *The Great Gatsby* and his wife, to whom he dedicated the book, are buried together under the classic's final line.

## FUNNY EPITAPHS

There are many people who decided their tombstone was the perfect chance to get in one last joke. In fact, some of the most famous funny epitaphs honor those who were not well-known in life. If you want to live on as an internet meme or listicle entry, start working on your best postmortem one-liner now.

> "That's all, folks."
>
> —MEL BLANC

Mel Blanc was the voice of many Looney Tunes characters, including Porky Pig, whose famous catchphrase serves as his epitaph.

"Here lies John Yeast. Pardon me for not rising."

—JOHN YEAST

While nothing else is known about the person buried under this gravestone, not even his birth or death dates, you can visit him at the Ruidoso-Hondo Valley Memorial Park in New Mexico.

"Jack Lemmon in"

—JACK LEMMON

This actor chose a visual joke for his epitaph that's meant to look like a film credit.

"Here lies Lester Moore. Four slugs from a 44. No Les. No more."

—LESTER MOORE

From the famous Wild West town of Tombstone, Arizona, Moore was supposedly killed in an argument over a badly mangled package. There's some doubt over whether Lester Moore ever existed, but don't let this stop you from being inspired by his hilarious epitaph. Johnny Cash certainly was—he included it as the opening lyrics to his song "The Ballad of Boot Hill."

"There goes the neighborhood."

—RODNEY DANGERFIELD

The famous comic was buried under a famous line from one of his famous jokes: "I tell ya I get no respect from anyone. I bought a cemetery plot. The guy said, 'There goes the neighborhood!'"

"I will not be right back after this message."

—MERV GRIFFIN

The host of multiple television shows waited his whole life to get this line in.

# UNIQUE EPITAPHS

You can think even further outside the box. People have used their epitaphs for all kinds of surprising purposes: to record a recipe, express a final grudge, preemptively curse those who tamper with their grave, and more. See some of the most unique epitaphs ever written below.

> "3.14159265358979323846264338327950288"

—LUDOLPH VAN CEULEN

The German mathematician calculated pi to thirty-five decimal places, and his impressive feat was engraved on his tombstone when he died in 1610. The original slab has been lost, but it was replaced in 2000.

> "Good friend for Jesus sake forbear, / To dig the dust enclosed here. / Blessed be the man that spares these stones, / And cursed be he that moves my bones."

—WILLIAM SHAKESPEARE

It's not known if Shakespeare wrote his own epitaph, but it certainly has his dark humor.

> "Lost life by stab in falling on ink eraser, evading six young women trying to give him birthday kisses in office Metropolitan Life Building."

—GEORGE SPENCER MILLET

This epitaph describes the bizarre accidental death of George Spencer Millet, who in 1909 fell on his ink eraser (a sharp tool, not the rubber kind) when being chased by his female coworkers.

# My PERFECT MONUMENT

Would you like to be memorialized for all time by a plaque, headstone, mausoleum, or something else entirely? How should this monument to you look?

Once you've figured that out, what should your epitaph be? If you're quoting someone else, or a religious text, double-check that you actually have the quote right and that the source is accurate. There is no backspace button on granite. Besides your epitaph and personal details, are there any artistic or design elements you would like included?

Here's a template to get you started. If you're not the artistic type, you can describe your dream monument in the space below. Be sure to include important logistical details, including where you would like your monument to be and the material it should be made from.

Or, if you're thinking something a lot bigger or less mainstream,* use this space to channel your inner Michelangelo. If you want anything particularly grand or quirky, make sure your chosen location will be cool with your unique vision. Some cemeteries and memorial parks are all about simplicity and uniformity.

---

\* While it's fun to dream about Italian marble and long quotes about the frailty of human existence that will bring any reader to tears for centuries to come, the reality is that funerary monuments are super expensive. That's why so many headstones look alike and are relatively simple. Be sure to look into prices before settling on your final design.

# FAMOUS GRAVESIDE RITUALS

**H**umans are obsessed with celebrities while they're alive, so why should we stop stanning them once they are dead? You'll probably never get within six feet of your favorite living famous person, but once they are in a grave, you can get even closer and there's nothing they can do about it (okay, fine, unless they're in a private cemetery). To honor the stars they adore, people have come up with a variety of creative, touching, and downright inappropriate graveside rituals.

## LIPSTICK KISSES ON OSCAR WILDE'S GRAVE

The Irish playwright's final resting place can be found in Paris, and for years, you couldn't miss it. It was the giant monument covered in lipstick. In the late 1990s, a mourner decided to plant a smacker on the tomb, and others followed suit. Eventually, Wilde's grave was covered. It got regular cleanings to wash the smooches off, but the grease from the cosmetics caused the stone to start wearing away. It got to the point that even Wilde's grandson said it was a "serious problem." Despite officials begging people to stop and even imposing a €9,000 fine if caught, fans kept up the kissing. In 2011, in desperation, the cemetery installed a glass barrier around the tomb.

## POTATOES AT FREDERICK THE GREAT'S GRAVE

It took 205 years for the eighteenth-century Prussian ruler to get the burial he asked for—a simple one at his summer palace, beside his dogs. Since the final time he was laid to rest, in 1991, visitors to his grave have left potatoes. Fredrick popularized the potato in Prussia at a time when more popular foodstuffs were in short supply due to famine. His fifteen decrees encouraging potato consumption and other efforts to make it acceptable to eat this food from the "heathen Americas" saved a lot of people from starvation. Still, he was a king, so he'd probably prefer that his mourners left caviar.

## THE BROKEN WAND CEREMONY AT HARRY HOUDINI'S GRAVE

Mourners leave lots of trinkets at the American escapologist's massive tombstone in Queens, New York, particularly playing cards, as a nod to his profession. But on his death in 1926, the magic community came up with an enduring tradition, one they repeat annually at Houdini's grave to this day and now perform for other deceased magicians. It's called the broken wand ceremony. A person breaks a wand over the grave while speaking these words: "Now its power is gone. It is a mere stick. Devoid of all meaning and authority. Useless without your hand to wield it." So many people started showing up to Houdini's broken wand ceremony over the years that the event had to be moved from Halloween (the anniversary of his death) to early November.

## "INDECENT RUBBING" AT VICTOR NOIR'S GRAVE

This probably isn't a name you know, but Noir, a French journalist who died in 1870 (in a duel, like a badass), somehow ended up with one of the weirdest graveside rituals. His tomb is beautiful, covered in a detailed bronze statue of him lying as if on his deathbed. In the 1970s, a rumor started that rubbing the bulge in the anatomically correct statue's trousers would bring good luck, or fertility for women who wanted a baby. Noir's groin is now a shiny copper color, whereas the rest of the statue is green with age. Attempts to stop the rubbing in 2004 failed (people protested until the fence that been constructed around the grave was removed), so visitors are still doing it today. In a sprawling cemetery with dozens of famous residents (Père Lachaise, in Paris), Noir's is the third-most-visited tomb, proving a good graveside ritual can earn you posthumous fame.

## THE POE TOASTER AT
## EDGAR ALLAN POE'S GRAVE

Edgar Allan Poe died in 1849 and was originally buried in a Baltimore cemetery, where there's now a memorial tombstone. Beginning about a hundred years later (no one is exactly sure when this started), a mysterious stranger would visit the site on the American poet's birthday, January 19, and drink a toast to Poe's memory, then leave a half-empty bottle of cognac on the grave, along with three roses. This ritual was first reported in the media in 1950, and after that, people often turned up to watch for "the Poe Toaster." He would sometimes leave notes as well, which were mostly odes to how awesome Edgar Allan Poe was. In 1993, he left a note explaining that he was going to pass the torch. Then, in 1999, a note revealed that the original Poe Toaster had died the year before and his son was taking over. But this son left opinions about sports and politics in his notes, which didn't go over well with locals or Poe fans. When a group tried to apprehend him at the graveyard in 2006, he got away, but he returned only three more times before the tradition ended as mysteriously as it had begun. Fortunately, in 2016 the Maryland Historical Society selected a new Poe Toaster to keep the tradition alive.

## "I VOTED" STICKERS
## ON SUSAN B. ANTHONY'S GRAVE

The great suffragist voted just once, in 1872, illegally. She was arrested and fined for daring to cast a vote while in possession of lady parts. Anthony would die well before the Nineteenth Amendment was passed in 1920, but since at least 2016, women have been thanking her by adorning her Rochester, New York, gravestone with the "I Voted" stickers they received after casting their ballots. Although the practice may have predated 2016, the ritual exploded into the mainstream the first year women could vote for a woman presidential candidate from a major political party. Eyewitnesses observing the phenomenon live on Election Day tweeted "the people keep coming" and that it was an "amazing sight." The tradition seems to be . . . sticking around, with crowds showing up again at the 2018 midterm elections. By 2020, the cemetery knew what was coming and installed a plastic shield over the grave so people could stick away without damaging the stone.

# My GRAVESIDE RITUAL

Humans love rituals. They help us feel in control, especially during anxiety-inducing situations, and visiting a loved one's resting place will probably bring on some level of anxiety in most people. So by leaving loved ones a ritual to take part in, even a silly or small one, you're helping them deal with the emotional effects of their loss.

And no matter what you come up with, there's probably a weirder tradition out there. If you want a flash mob to perform an intricately choreographed interpretive dance to Adele's "Someone Like You" ever year on the anniversary of your death, go for it. (Just understand it might happen once—at best—before your loved ones conveniently "forget" and never speak of it again.) Even a simple ritual can be effective, such as asking your spouse to always wear the shirt you liked best on them when they come visit you.

Use the space below to describe the traditions would you like performed at your graveside.

# FAMADIHANA

In parts of Madagascar, death is no excuse to stop partying with your family. Millions of the island's citizens participate in *famadihana*, also known as "the turning of the bones." While, yes, technically the bones do get turned, first they are danced around with to live music and spoken to and generally shown a great time at a *very* extended family reunion, one that reaches right through the veil of death.

The famadihana occurs every five to seven years. The period varies because it's the dead who decide when it's time. An ancestor may appear to a senior family member in a dream, saying they are "cold and need new clothes." Then the family will get everyone together, open the crypt, and take out the bodies. After the deceased are rewrapped in new shrouds, family members dance around with the bodies on their shoulders. When carrying the corpse of Grandma gets tiring, a person might ask her for good health or good fortune. And there's lots of drinking and feasting, although that part the late ancestors don't partake in. Finally, the bodies are sealed back up until the next time one of them gets a bit chilly.

While religious beliefs in Madagascar vary, everyone can agree that famadihana brings people together. But in other parts of the world, if your grandkids take you out of your tomb, it will be considered grave robbing. And the cops are not going to believe they were just bringing you to a party. Still, it's nice to imagine what could be possible.

# EXTRAORDINARY CEMETERIES YOU NEED TO VISIT (BEFORE YOU END UP IN ONE)

**V**isiting cemeteries might be something you associate with your high-school goth phase, but there are some incredible ones that you can visit for inspiration before you die and, if you are lucky, maybe relocate to after.

## THE MERRY CEMETERY, ROMANIA

Cemeteries aren't usually associated with merriment, but the name of this one in Romania isn't a mistranslation. The place is home to over 800 brightly colored wooden tombstones, which are crammed with visual and written jokes and poems and scenes from the lives of the deceased. One shows the town drunk being pulled into the grave by a skeleton as he enjoys his last drink. One man's epitaph reminds the reader that he loved other men's wives, and another implores you not to wake the woman buried below, lest she come back and scold her son-in-law.

## HOLLYWOOD FOREVER CEMETERY, UNITED STATES

Everything in Hollywood is cool, including the place where its dead are buried. So many famous people are buried at Hollywood Forever that the *Washington Post* recommends you skip the Walk of Fame and go to the cemetery instead. Famous and infamous residents include rocker Johnny Ramone, director Cecil B. DeMille, actress and singer Judy Garland, gangster Bugsy Siegel, voice actor Mel Blanc (who's also the owner of one great epitaph; see page 133), and actress and TV host Maila Nurmi (otherwise known as Vampira). The cemetery even hosts concerts and movie nights for the living.

## THE CATACOMBS OF PARIS, FRANCE

In the late eighteenth century, the City of Lights had a problem. Real estate was getting hard to find. Not for the living, but for the dead. By that point, people had been dying there for thousands of years, and the churchyards were full to bursting—literally. It was a public health crisis that was solved by digging up older remains and moving them to a massive underground quarry full of tunnels that was, at the time, located outside the city limits. Bones were piled up by the millions, skulls staring out at anyone who dared venture below. These days, more than half a million tourists a year do dare, and hopefully find some macabre beauty in all the bones.

## LA RECOLETA CEMETERY, ARGENTINA

This Buenos Aires cemetery is more like a thriving city for dead people than your standard burial place. Each body gets its own above-ground mausoleum, which look like houses lining narrow streets. No two mausoleums are alike, and most are elaborately decorated with stone columns, statues, and friezes. And don't cry for Eva "Evita" Peron, Argentina (or any other country). As of 1976, after a mysterious and controversial twenty-year postmortem journey round the world, she's spending her afterlife in this fabulous necropolis, in a crypt that the BBC described in 2012 as "fortified like a nuclear bunker" to keep ghoulish souvenir hunters out.

## OKUNOIN CEMETERY, JAPAN

The largest cemetery in Japan is also a UNESCO World Heritage Site. It's not hard to see why. Besides being 1,200 years old, it's home to over 100 Buddhist and Shinto temples and more than 200,000 tombstones. One of the perks of working for a company in Japan could be the right to have your ashes interred in their official Okunoin plot, often marked by a memorial related to the job, like a 15-foot rocket or a large stone coffee cup. There are even monuments to dead termites and pufferfish. Not to mention a mausoleum with 10,000 lamps that are permanently lit and thousands of Buddha statues, many of which are dressed in red beanies and bibs by people looking to accrue merit for the afterlife.

## GREYFRIARS KIRKYARD, SCOTLAND

If you're only interested in going to graveyards for the chance of a ghost encounter, then Edinburgh has the one for you. Known as one of—if not *the*—most haunted cemeteries in the world, by 2006 there had been 450 documented "attacks" by angry spirits and 140 people who have fainted on its grounds. There's also a statue of Greyfriars Bobby, a dog that was said to have laid on his master's grave until his own death fourteen years later. Harry Potter fans will appreciate that J. K. Rowling wrote the first book in the series in a café down the street from Greyfriars, and a grave in the cemetery bears the name of one Thomas Riddell.

# Obituaries

Once you are dead, your friends and family will often find they need to sum you up in just a few words. This might be in a eulogy, to their therapist, or in your obituary. The latter is a particular art. Whereas a eulogy is delivered at the funeral and can be as long as you or the speaker wants, obits usually run in newspapers or other publications that charge by the line—so they tend to be shorter (unless you choose to publish online). It's nearly impossible to sum up a whole life in a few dozen sentences, to get in the big achievements and the little quirks that made the person special, plus all the other standard information expected in an obituary. Fortunately, whether you leave the task to a loved one or write it yourself, there are plenty of amazing obituaries out there to draw inspiration from.

One of the oldest known obituaries, written in Greek on a limestone tablet and discovered in Egypt, memorializes a regular woman who lived roughly 1,700 years ago:

*"In peace and blessing, Ama Helene, a Jew, who loves the orphans, [died]. For about sixty years her path was one of mercy and blessing; on it she prospered."*

Frida Kahlo was a victim of postmortem sexism in a 1954 Associated Press obituary (proving that it's especially wise for women to write their own obits):

*"Frida Kahlo, wife of Diego Rivera, the noted painter, was found dead in her home today. . . . She was also a painter . . ."*

The 2015 obituary of Douglas Legler in the *Forum of Fargo-Moorhead* was as to-the-point as it gets, saying, in total:

*"Doug died."*

(This was not due to uncaring next of kin.
In life, Legler requested that exact obituary "over and over.")

In his 2013 *Columbus Dispatch* obituary,
Scott E. Entsminger got one final dig in:

"A lifelong Cleveland Browns fan and season ticket holder,
he also wrote a song each year and sent it to the Cleveland
Browns as well as offering other advice on how to run the team.
He respectfully requests six Cleveland Browns pall bearers so
the Browns can let him down one last time."

According to her 2015 *Florida Times Union* obituary,
Emily DeBrayda Phillips wasn't surprised by her fate:

"It pains me to admit it, but apparently, I have passed away.
Everyone told me it would happen one day but that's simply
not something I wanted to hear, much less experience.
Once again I didn't get things my way! That's been the
story of my life all my life."

Good news: we finally know the secret identity of Spider-Man.
Bad news: he's dead, as reported in Aaron Joseph Purmort's 2014
obituary in Minnesota's *Star Tribune.*

"Aaron Joseph Purmort, age 35, died peacefully at home on
November 25 after complications from a radioactive spider
bite that led to years of crime-fighting and a years-long battle
with a nefarious criminal named Cancer, who has plagued
our society for far too long. Civilians will recognize him best
as Spider-Man, and thank him for his many years of service
protecting our city."

Val Patterson finally came clean in his 2012 obituary in the *Salt Lake Tribune*:

"Now that I have gone to my reward, I have confessions and
things I should now say. As it turns out, I AM the guy who stole
the safe from the Motor View Drive Inn back in June 1971. I could
have left that unsaid, but I wanted to get it off my chest. Also, I
really am NOT a PhD. What happened was that the day I went

*to pay off my college student loan at the U of U, the girl working there put my receipt into the wrong stack, and two weeks later, a PhD diploma came in the mail. I didn't even graduate, I only had about 3 years of college credit. In fact, I never did even learn what the letters 'PhD' even stood for."*

In this 2013 *Sun Herald* obituary, the family of Harry Stamps had one final request on his behalf:

*"Finally, the family asks that in honor of Harry that you write your Congressman and ask for the repeal of Day Light Saving Time. Harry wanted everyone to get back on the Lord's Time."*

According to his 2013 *Savannah Morning News* obituary, William "Freddie" McCullough died as he lived: a teller of tall tales.

*"Freddie was killed when he rushed into a burning orphanage to save a group of adorable children. Or maybe not. We all know how he liked to tell stories."*

## WRITING YOUR OWN OBIT: *Having the Last Word*

While some people refuse to accept that they will die one day and would never write a postmortem tribute to themselves, others weigh their fear of death against their fear that some relative will write a crappy CliffNotes version of their life and put it in the paper for everyone to read. It's a valid concern.

Even when you write it yourself, obituaries are usually in the third person, though they don't have to be. If you want to speak directly to your reader, use first person. You can be funny, self-deprecating, and a little out there. Or follow the standard form: name and dates, a straightforward chronology of your life, when and how you died, who survived and predeceased you, where your services will be held, and where flowers or donations can be sent (although someone else will probably have to fill in those last bits for you). What matters most is that your obituary is a reflection of you.

# My OBITUARY

Try out a few different tones and ideas. Don't worry about getting it right on the first try. It's hard to cover your whole life and personality in just a few words. You can keep tweaking it until it's perfect . . . or until you die. Whichever comes first.

# Your Material Legacy

Most people don't leave behind just their bodies when they die, but lots and lots of stuff, too. Even if you never ended up on the show *Hoarders*, chances are you have a closet or an attic or a garage that is filled to the brim with material possessions. At some point you've probably tried to do a clear-out, only to hold up some random object and ask, "Why do I have *this*?"

Once you are dead, your loved ones will have to go through all that accumulated junk. But, hidden among the broken toaster you were totally going to fix one day and the guitar you were totally going to learn how to play are things of great worth. Whether they are sentimental or hold monetary value or both, these things are your material legacy. (Not to mention any cash you have stashed in your accounts or under your mattress, plus bigger assets like a house or car.)

While your material legacy may not be as important as the legacy of your intangible essence (at least, that's what we're supposed to say, isn't it?), it's still very important to get it in order and plan who gets what and in what amount. Unless you plan on taking it all to the grave with you like an ancient emperor or pharaoh, the stuff you leave behind needs to be sorted out before you die, both physically and metaphorically.

Also consider anything you have that you might not want the wrong relative stumbling upon after your death. Like that gimp suit you can't be cremated in. Or maybe you have a document lying around that contains a secret you plan on taking to your grave. Don't let your years of living under the crushing weight of that secret be in vain by letting your family discover it immediately after your death. Consider keeping anything extra sensitive in a home safe or bank safe-deposit box. You can go a step further and leave instructions for the items to be destroyed rather than passed on.

# GETTING YOUR STUFF IN ORDER

Whether you have a complicated estate of millions of dollars and lots of property, or a few belongings and some debt to leave behind, it's important to know what your material legacy will look like and to plan accordingly. Who will be willed what in your will? Who very specifically will *not* be getting anything? Getting your affairs in order means getting your stuff in order, too.

Would you like your money to be donated to a certain charity or organization in honor of your life? What does this particular organization mean to you?

Are there any special family keepsakes you'd like to pass on? Other than money, the stuff your loved ones are most likely to fight over are family keepsakes. Of course, it's nice to believe they'll be calm and rational about it, but material things, especially expensive ones, can make even the nicest people go a bit crazy. Throw in the emotional weight of family heirlooms and you can have a disaster on your hands. So when naming who you want to get what (see "Who Gets My Stuff," page 154), consider saying *why* you think each person deserves this special something particularly. It will mean more to the recipient, and anyone who is disappointed will at least understand your reasons.

Who are the candidates to be your executors (the people who are charged with carrying out your will)? Make sure you talk to them about taking on the job. It can be a difficult task, and not everyone is up to it. Putting a little something extra in your will for them can make it that much easier.

And just to be clear, the worksheet on page 154 IS NOT YOUR WILL. While it's good to get your thoughts together here, and it can informally help your family when it is time, be very aware this has no legal standing and you need to make an actual will, for many, many reasons (see "Where There's a Will," page 155).

# WHO GETS *my* STUFF

Consider the various property you will leave behind, whether it be sentimental trinkets or larger assets like a house, car, or the contents of your bank account. You can leave whatever you like to whomever you like, whether that's your children, favorite charity, or beloved barber. Express your wishes and explain your reasoning for each decision below. Include special considerations, including who you would like to be your executor, in the notes section.

**I WOULD LIKE** _____ **TO HAVE** _____

**BECAUSE** _____.

**I WOULD LIKE** _____ **TO HAVE** _____

**BECAUSE** _____.

**I WOULD LIKE** _____ **TO HAVE** _____

**BECAUSE** _____.

**I WOULD LIKE** _____ **TO HAVE** _____

**BECAUSE** _____.

**NOTES** ...........................................................................

.............................................................................................

.............................................................................................

.............................................................................................

.............................................................................................

.............................................................................................

.............................................................................................

# Where There's a Will

You've spent all this time planning. You've looked deep into your soul and envisioned the perfect way for your loved ones to say goodbye to you. These preparations will help you face death with less fear, because you know what will happen after you are gone. Or . . . do you? After all, you will be dead. What's to stop your loved ones from saying "Screw it!" and doing their own thing, regardless of your wishes? Unfortunately, not a whole lot.

However, there are some safeguards you can take. One very smart thing to do is prearrange everything yourself. That means finding a funeral home, crematory, or other relevant business for whatever you want done to your body and working with them now. In some cases you can even prepay at today's prices for the services, no matter when you end up dying. Considering the skyrocketing costs of funerals year-on-year, this could end up saving you (or your family) a lot of money, not to mention preparation time.

While you have some control over what happens to your body, the rest of your funeral details are harder to guarantee. Another approach is to tell everyone what you want now, convince them of anything they might be unsure about, and make sure you explain your reasoning clearly using the worksheets in this book. That way, all your careful planning is more likely to come to fruition. Being open and honest about your wishes, and making them known to your friends as well as family, means no one can say, "Oh, he wanted his ashes shot into space? I thought he'd be fine being buried in this very boring cemetery in the middle of nowhere."

Your other option is to record your wishes in your will, which essentially means tying your postmortem plans and dreams to your money. Think: "I leave my entire estate to my beloved son, on the condition that he cremate me and spread my ashes to the wind from the top of the Eiffel Tower." Talk to a lawyer about your ideas. There are ways to help ensure the send-off you want, but it's best to work with a professional to make sure it's all legally binding. But that's not the only reason to write a will. Some people are superstitious about wills, as if they'll make one and immediately keel over once they sign it. (Or as if someone in the will, perhaps the secret nemesis they don't know they have, will decide to off them to get theirs quicker.) That almost never happens. What does happen all the time is that people die without a will and all hell breaks loose. Sure, you'll be dead, so it's not your problem, but if you want to ensure things go smoothly after you die, write the freaking will.

Even the most loving family can be ripped apart over who gets what or who gets to plan the funeral or who becomes the guardian of children or pets. The stress of a death makes the people left behind angry and irrational. The courts are full of families fighting over inheritances. Charles Dickens wrote a whole book about it (*Bleak House*), recounting how a family fought for so long over an inheritance that they blew all the money on lawyers. The novel was a satirical take on a real court case, because when it comes to trying to get their hands on some cash, some people will do almost anything. And it might not be clear who those people are until after you are dead.

Recording everything in this book is a great first step, but now you need to make it legal. You don't even need to pay a lawyer. Websites like Willing.com can make the process simple for you. (Unless you have a huge, complicated estate, in which case you can probably afford a fancy lawyer just fine, Mr. Bezos.) And once you have the will? For the love of God, keep it someplace safe and fireproof, and make sure the right people know what that place is. The only thing worse than dying with no will is dying with a will everyone knows you have but no one can find.

# MONTH'S MIND

The Month's Mind originated in Scandinavia, where the Vikings held ceremonial drinking events for the somewhat-recently dead, which just sounds like an excuse to get drunk. It caught on in England by the 600s, but Christianity took the alcohol out of the gatherings and adapted the tradition into a requiem mass and feast held one month after a person's death. That didn't mean things couldn't still get a bit crazy, though. The 1926 edition of the *Encyclopedia Britannica* recorded one Thomas Windsor (died 1479) who left instructions that included rounding up one hundred children to sing for his soul at his Month's Mind.

Eventually, the practice caught on in Ireland and is still commonly practiced there by Catholics. These days, most Catholics outside Ireland have never heard of this religious tradition, but it's making a comeback. And Month's Minds are a great idea. Funerals usually take place relatively soon after a death, and loved ones are often still shell-shocked. Since a funeral brings a sense of finality to a lot of people, those closest to the deceased may find themselves on their own when they finally start the grieving process. Getting everyone together a month later for mass and a meal, or even just holding a special service for all members of the community who have died that month, is a way of acknowledging that the deceased, and their loved ones, are not forgotten.

# Your Digital Legacy

Living on online may be even more important than the stuff you leave behind. So much of our lives are virtual, and since we're supposed to be extra-super-secret with our passwords and protections, when you die your family will probably discover they have no way of accessing anything of yours in the digital realm. Often it's just a minor inconvenience, but sometimes it will be a big deal. What if they need important details like your bank accounts or a legal document? What auto-pay charges will need to be canceled? What if there are photos or videos that only you had access to? Your social media accounts will need to be shut down or turned into memorial pages. There are a million miscellaneous digital items that could suddenly become really important—and really inaccessible.

There are work-arounds: your family might be able to present other forms of identification to gain access, or they could ask a tween nephew to hack into your accounts. But these take time and effort (and may land the tween in legal hot water). You will save your loved ones additional pain and suffering by leaving behind your passwords, answers to security questions, and other pertinent information for any business that will be left undone with your passing.

Make sure to cover everything, from social media to email to banking to your Etsy store (see "My Digital Assets," opposite). Due to privacy laws, your inheritors may not be able to access all of your digital accounts unless you expressly give permission in your will, so don't neglect digital assets when drawing one up.

The worst-case scenario is becoming disturbingly common: people trying to use a dead person's finger or face to open their phone. This doesn't always work, depending on the type of technology and how long the person has been dead. In 2018, police stormed into a Florida funeral home and tried to open a phone seized as evidence using a corpse's fingerprint, but failed. The FBI admits they have attempted it. Don't make your loved ones have to try this. Just leave them your passwords.

Oh, and just as with your material legacy, consider any sensitive things you might not want certain relatives to stumble on after you die. They'll thank you for saving them the shock and pain.

# My DIGITAL ASSETS

Write down your credentials for accounts your next of kin will need to access after you are gone.* Use the instructions section to record your wishes, including what you would like done with the digital asset, file paths to important photos, who you'd like to manage the asset, etc.

**DIGITAL ASSET:** _____

**USERNAME:** _____ **PASSWORD:** _____

**INSTRUCTIONS:** _____

_____

**DIGITAL ASSET:** _____

**USERNAME:** _____ **PASSWORD:** _____

**INSTRUCTIONS:** _____

_____

**DIGITAL ASSET:** _____

**USERNAME:** _____ **PASSWORD:** _____

**INSTRUCTIONS:** _____

_____

**DIGITAL ASSET:** _____

**USERNAME:** _____ **PASSWORD:** _____

**INSTRUCTIONS:** _____

_____

---

\*  It's a million times more likely that your passwords will be hacked through a security breach on your computer than by someone stealing this book and reading this page. But in any case, keep this book in a safe place.

# Your Intangible Legacy

You are more than just the body you will leave behind. More than the items listed in your will. More than the stories people will tell about you. You are an infinitely complex being. The chances of you ever existing are so miniscule, your life could be considered a miracle. Faced with thousands of decisions every day, and a lot of luck and coincidence, you built a full and meaningful life. No one will ever live one like it again. You are unique, in all of the 13.7 billion years since the universe began. When you are no more, it will be impossible for anyone to really understand your whole essence, because it took a full lifetime to create.

But that doesn't mean you can't try to explain it.

"What you leave behind is not what is engraved in stone monuments, but what is woven into the lives of others."

—PERICLES, ANCIENT GREEK STATESMAN AND ORATOR

# TEN THINGS I'M PROUD
## of ACCOMPLISHING

They say pride comes before a fall, but the fall we're talking about here is death, and that is coming one way or another, so screw it. Be proud. You've done amazing things in your life, hundreds if not thousands of notable, caring, impressive things, and narrowing those down to just ten is going to be hard. Society teaches us to downplay our accomplishments, but this is not the moment for false modesty or being hard on yourself. Think back on all the things you've done that make you proud. Maybe it's getting a promotion, raising great kids, rescuing an animal, or writing a book. Maybe there are things that seem small, like acing a hard test in high school or comforting a friend when they were upset. Nothing is too minor to include. This is a map of the best parts of your soul.

1 _____

2 _____

3 _____

4 _____

5 _____

6 _____

7 _____

8 _____

9 _____

10 _____

# Coming Back to Haunt Someone

Most ghost stories involve strangers' spirits. As in, a couple moves into a spooky old house, or kids chant some words in front of mirror, and suddenly a scary ghost is there—but it's not the incorporeal figure of someone familiar. Figuring out who the ghost is and what their back story is is half the fun of the haunting.

But that doesn't mean you can't come back to haunt those you know. The ancient Greeks used to keep their ancestors happy by throwing a feast every year, inviting their ghosts to attend, and then very firmly telling them to leave until the next party. Consider asking your relatives to gather for a big annual shindig and promise to grace it with your ghostly presence.

When people claim to see the ghosts of relatives, often the story is sweet rather than scary. After an initial shock—because, you know, there's a dead person floating around—the encounter is usually reassuring, with the ghost telling their loved one that it's okay they are dead. While this may say more about the psychological needs of grieving people, maybe spirits really do have the option of popping back in to visit the folks who've survived them. Think about doing it yourself if you get the chance.

# My HAUNTING GAME PLAN

Use this space to draw the ghostly form you will take after death, so that after you return from the grave, your hauntees will know it's you. There are poltergeists, ghostly mists, glowing orbs, funnel ghosts, and your traditional ghost apparitions. Or you could be something less ethereal, returning in the form of a bird, butterfly, or rainbow.

While you could, of course, use this opportunity to terrorize your nemesis, ghostly hauntings don't have to be scary. Instead, you can use your spirit form to lovingly float in and out of someone's life. Use the lines beside your drawing to describe whom you will haunt (or merely watch over), how, and why.

# A MESSAGE to my LOVED ONES

No jokes here. You may think you'll have time to say all the things you want to, all the things the people close to you need to hear. You may think you'll have the cinematic deathbed scene where you say your last "I love you"s and unburden yourself with your final confessions before you pass on. In reality, the chances are slim you'll go out that way, and it's much more likely you'll miss your last chance to express what you want to.

Leave a message here for your loved ones to read after you are gone. Loving, poignant, angry, whatever you need to tell them. Imagine being in that movie-style deathbed scene. What do you want to say?

# How to Craft a Bucket List

In the 1800s, the philosopher William James said the knowledge that we must die is "the worm at the core" of human existence. In a book of the same name, authors Sheldon Solomon, Jeff Greenberg, and Tom Pyszczynski studied research showing that the knowledge of our inevitable demise, the constant, low-frequency buzzing in the back of our brains telling us each moment could be our last, actually drives both individuals and civilization forward. Death makes us want to be more alive.

That's where writing your bucket list comes in. Okay, yes, it's been made into a cliché by Hollywood, but at its core, the bucket list is an important exercise. In general, humans are bad at following through with things. (Has one of your New Year's resolutions *ever* lasted into February?) But research has shown again and again that people who write down their goals are more likely to achieve them.

If you're stuck, here are some of the top bucket list items, according to a 2017 survey by Match.com:

1. Fall in love

2. Go on a wine tour in Napa

3. Change someone's life for the better

4. Get to your ideal weight (*don't listen to the list, you are beautiful just as you are!*)

5. Go on a safari

6. Ride a hot air balloon

7. See the Northern Lights

8. Go to the Super Bowl

9. Swim with dolphins

10. Travel through Europe

# My BUCKET LIST

You've buckled down and done the work of confronting your mortality by reading this book—now take that knowledge, convert it into energy, and go achieve amazing things while you still can! Write your goals here—the more detail, the better. As in: You don't just want to swim with dolphins—you want to fly to the Dolphin Research Center in Florida, spend twenty-five minutes in the water during the Dolphin Encounter program, then buy a hand-painted dolphin tote from the gift shop. Now do the same for your nine other goals. (Or ten, if you don't want to swim with dolphins, but what kind of cynic doesn't want to swim with dolphins?!)

1 _____

2 _____

3 _____

4 _____

5 _____

6 _____

7 _____

8 _____

9 _____

10 _____

# EPILOGUE
## THE END OF THE BEGINNING OF YOUR END

In Bhutan, often rated the happiest nation in the world, it's considered important to reflect on death five times a day. The rest of the world would do well to learn from them. You've taken a huge step in reading and filling out this book—now it's time to finish the journey.

Continue to fine-tune your plans, both for your funeral and for the rest of your life. Think about death in a manner than will motivate you to live the best, most fulfilling life possible. The search for immortality drives many people, but the realization that there is an end to all this is equally inspiring. After all, everyone who looked for immortality failed. By preparing for death in a spiritual and physical way, you are ensuring that you will succeed right to the end.

This means you can't let those knuckleheads—the people you care about most in the world—screw it up for you. Since you will be unable to bring all your detailed and well-thought-out funeral plans to fruition yourself, you need to explain your wishes to your loved ones. And since the universe is unfair and vindictive with a sick sense of humor, you could be run over by a circus elephant tomorrow. Which means this isn't something you can put off: you need to tell them now.

They will almost certainly push back. People are scared to talk about death, as if speaking the words will make it so. They don't want to think about the reality that you will be gone one day, and, by logical extension, that they will be too. They will probably not come home from work on some random Tuesday ready to have a long, emotional chat with a side of existential crisis.

So your loved ones might need convincing, or you might need to make more than one attempt. You might have to explain death positivity and how planning your funeral makes you feel more in control of your life. That you're not being morbid or trying to upset them. If anything, you are planning ahead in order to help them in a trying time. Show them this book. Explain the meaning and thought behind your wishes. Eventually, all but the most stubborn of people—the ones who would have been slashing through the jungle, desperately searching for the fountain of youth—will realize the benefits. Maybe they will even want their own book to fill out.

I hope this has been an exciting journey, a meaningful reflection, and a laugh riot. Dying is scary and inevitable, so there's nothing more appropriate than to laugh right in its stupid, skeletal face.

One final note: What kind of funeral cake would you like? (I told you we were going to make this a thing. See page 51.)

# FURTHER READING

This book is only the first step into death positivity. If you have questions, want to know more, or just have a morbid fascination with this stuff, check out these works.

## THE PHILOSOPHY AND PSYCHOLOGY OF DEATH:

*How does dying help us live?*

*Immortality: The Quest to Live Forever and How It Drives Civilization* by Stephen Cave (New York: Skyhorse, 2017)

*The Worm at the Core: On the Role of Death in Life* by Jeff Greenberg, Sheldon Solomon, and Tom Pyszczynski (New York: Random House, 2015)

## THE SCIENCE OF DEATH:

*For when philosophy makes your head hurt too much*

*All that Remains: A Renowned Forensic Scientist on Death, Mortality, and Solving Crimes* by Sue Black (New York: Arcade Publishing, 2019)

*Stiff: The Curious Life of Human Cadavers* by Mary Roach (New York: W. W. Norton & Company, 2004)

## DEATH INDUSTRY PROFESSIONALS:

*Lessons and laughs from the people who have seen everything*

*Confessions of a Funeral Director: How the Business of Death Saved My Life* by Caleb Wilde (New York: HarperCollins, 2017)

*Curtains: Adventures of an Undertaker-in-Training* by Tom Jokinen (Cambridge: Da Capo Press, 2010)

*Life as a Casketeer: What the Business of Death Can Teach the Living* by Francis Tipen (New York: HarperCollins, 2021)

*Mortuary Confidential: Undertakers Spill the Dirt* by Kenneth McKenzie and Todd Harra (New York: Citadel Press, 2010)

*Smoke Gets in Your Eyes and Other Lessons from the Crematory* by Caitlin Doughty (New York: W. W. Norton & Company, 2015)

*The Undertaking: Life Studies from the Dismal Trade* by Thomas Lynch (New York: Penguin Books, 1998)

# YOU'VE GOT QUESTIONS, THEY'VE GOT ANSWERS:

*Tips, tricks, and advice from the experts*

*Advice for Future Corpses (and Those Who Love Them): A Practical Perspective on Death and Dying* by Sallie Tisdale (New York: Gallery Books, 2019)

*Does This Mean You'll See Me Naked?: Field Notes from a Funeral Director* by Robert Webster (Naperville: Sourcebooks, 2011)

*Do I Have to Wear Black to a Funeral?: 112 Etiquette Guidelines for the New Rules of Death* by Florence Isaacs (New York: The Countryman Press, 2020)

*Reimagining Death: Stories and Practical Wisdom for Home Funerals and Green Burials* by Lucinda Herring (Berkeley: North Atlantic Books, 2019)

*Will My Cat Eat My Eyeballs?: Big Questions from Tiny Mortals About Death* by Caitlin Doughty (New York: W. W. Norton & Company, 2020)

# HISTORY AND CULTURE:

*Learning about death across time and space*

*The American Way of Death Revisited* by Jessica Mitford (New York: Vintage Books, 2000)

*Death and the Afterlife: A Chronological Journey, from Cremation to Quantum Resurrection* by Clifford A. Pickover (New York: Sterling, 2015)

*Disconnected from Death: The Evolution of Funerary Customs & the Unmasking of Death in America* by April Slaughter and Troy Taylor (Jacksonville: American Hauntings Ink, 2018)

*From Here to Eternity: Traveling the World to Find the Good Death* by Caitlin Doughty (New York: W. W. Norton & Company, 2018)

*The History of Death* by Michael Kerrigan (London: Amber Books, 2017)

*Near the Exit: Travels with the Not-So-Grim Reaper* by Lori Erickson (Louisville: Westminster John Knox Press, 2019)

*The Victorian Book of the Dead* by Chris Woodyard (Dayton: Kestrel Publications, 2014)

*The Whole Death Catalog: A Lively Guide to the Bitter End* by Harold Schechter (New York: Ballantine Books, 2009)

# INDEX

# ACKNOWLEDGMENTS

Writing a book about accepting the inevitability of death in the middle of a once-in-a-century pandemic was a mental and emotional minefield. But despite what the universe threw at all of us in 2020, this book was an absolute dream to write, and so many people made it happen.

Thank you, first and foremost, to Rebecca Gyllenhaal. You and everyone at Quirk were so helpful. I hope this final product exceeded the expectations of your original idea. Thank you for trusting me with it, and for tolerating the many, many emails and DMs I sent you over the last year. And thank you for being flexible on deadlines when the news of the day would make writing jokes about funerals impossible.

My amazing agent Melissa Gaines, as well as Shannon Orso and Lizz Nagle at Victress Literary: you are rock stars. Thank you for the insane amount of work you do, and for replying to my endless messages day and night.

To my husband, Simon, who is the best editor I know, thank you for reading everything I threw at you and for always being both painfully honest and my biggest cheerleader. Thank you also to my mother and father (Mommy and Daddy), who read early drafts. (And Mommy, thank you for taking me to that secluded Airbnb with the amazing view of Lake Travis so I could safely get away and write. I didn't actually write a word in the end, but it was a much-needed vacation.) My sister Lisa, I'm still waiting for your edits on that draft I sent you in July, but I won't hold that against you for the rest of your life. Thank you for helping me out with the podcast. I'll make sure your eulogy mentions what a sexy beast you were, as requested.

Thank you to Sylvie for all our check-ins and motivational phone calls. You kept me going.

A big thanks to all the people who let me talk at them about death and funerals, whether it was in person or online. I love how many of us are weird in the same ways.

And finally, thank you to my perfect fur baby, Briscoe. I am sorry I bought your nemesis (the laptop) to write this book, thus depriving you of your rightful place, my lap, for short periods of time. I know how badly you suffered, and I will make it up to you with the biggest monument a pet cemetery has ever seen.